CAROL TENNANT

Book of

Preserves

WOMEN'S INSTITUTE

SIMON &
SCHUSTER

NEW YORK · SYDNEY · TORONTO

Acknowledgements

Thanks to Mrs Sheila Bishop, NFWI cookery and preserves judge, lead tutor
for judges training and member of Worcestershire Federation.

First published in Great Britain by Simon & Schuster UK Ltd, 2008
Paperback edition 2009
A CBS Company

Simon & Schuster UK Ltd
222 Gray's Inn Road, London WC1X 8HB

1 3 5 7 9 10 8 6 4 2

Design: Fiona Andreanelli (www.andreanelli.com)
Food photography: Ian Garlick (www.garlickfood.com)
Stylist for food photography: Liz Belton

Printed and bound in China

ISBN 978-1-84737-176-8 hardback
ISBN 978-1-84737-177-5 paperback

Contents

Introduction

We've been preserving fruit, vegetables, meat and fish for many hundreds of years because the short shelf life of many foods and the lack of cold storage made preserving a necessity. The advent of refrigeration and airfreight has meant that we no longer need to preserve food for lean times. Now, we preserve things simply because we've come to enjoy eating them.

There are a variety of methods of preserving food for long periods. These include using sugar, salt or vinegar as preservatives, or smoking, drying and freezing, though some of these methods are less well suited to a domestic environment. This book contains recipes for sugar, vinegar and dried preserves, plus a couple of sauces and jams that can be frozen.

Preserving with sugar is a method we use for preserving fruit in season. Sugar preserves include jams, jellies, marmalades, conserves and compôtes. If the concentration of sugar is high enough in a preserve, it prevents micro-organisms from thriving and reproducing. You'll find all the usual recipes in this book –

Strawberry Jam, Damson Jam, Seville Orange Marmalade – plus variations on these to create a variety of other classics. There are more unusual combinations, too, including Raspberry and lime jam, Blueberry and lemon jam, Apricot and ginger conserve and Strawberry vanilla compôte. I hope that these recipes will inspire you to create your own favourite combinations.

Preserving with vinegar is a method commonly used to preserve vegetables, though some fruits work very well in vinegar-based preserves. Vinegar preserves include chutneys, relishes and pickles. Chutneys are slow-cooked mixtures, usually of fruit and vegetables, with the addition of sugar and vinegar. Relishes usually contain less vinegar, are more coarsely chopped and don't require a period of maturation before they can be eaten. Pickles are generally whole vegetables or vegetables cut into large chunks, then preserved in flavoured vinegar. You will find all the classic pickles – Pickled gherkins, Pickled onions, Apple chutney, Sweet pickled beetroot – alongside some new favourites such as Orange pickle and Ratatouille relish.

You'll find recipes that make use of a wide range of ingredients, so whether you're shopping at your local greengrocer or supermarket, have an allotment or access to a local pick-your-own farm or farmers' market, you'll find a recipe to help you make the best of them.

Tips for Preserving

Sugar preserves

Sugar has long been used as a way of preserving fruit since it prevents micro-organisms from surviving – any that are present in a high sugar preserve will simply dry up and will therefore be unable to reproduce.

JAM is fruit and sugar cooked together until it reaches a gel consistency. Jam should be clear, well set but not stiff (it should be spreadable) with a distinctive fruity flavour and good colour.

CONSERVES are similar to jam, but the set tends to be softer. They usually also contain dried fruit and/or nuts.

JELLY does not use the whole fruit, just the juice. The whole fruit is gently cooked, then left to strain as long as overnight. The resulting juice is then boiled up with sugar until a set is reached. The yield of jellies is necessarily lower than that of jam, as the bulk of the fruit is not used.

MARMALADE has a similar consistency to jam but is made using citrus fruit and peel, though combinations of other fruits can also be used. Because it contains peel, it takes much longer to cook.

CURDS are not really preserves, as the addition of butter and eggs means they have a much shorter shelf life. But they will keep for 2 to 3 weeks in the refrigerator. Curds should be put into a warm jar and sealed with a waxed disc and covered with a cellophane cover.

FREEZER JAMS are made using uncooked fruit, a lot of sugar and commercial pectin. The jam retains the fresh flavour of the fruit – strawberry and raspberry are best, though peaches also make good freezer jam. Freezer jam keeps for up to 6 months in the freezer.

Vinegar preserves

The first that come to mind are pickles. A clear pickle is made by brining or salting vegetables to extract their excess water, which makes them very crisp. They are then packed in vinegar, which may or may not be spiced, sweet or otherwise flavoured.

SWEET PICKLES are made using sweet, usually spicy, vinegar in which the fruit or vegetables are stewed before being packed.

MIXED PICKLES are made when mixed vegetables are brined or salted before being cooked in thickened vinegar, usually with spices.

All vinegar preserves need to be covered with vinegar-proof lids – metal lids will rust and waxed discs or cellophane will allow the vinegar to evaporate.

CHUTNEY is a mixture of fruit and vegetables cooked with sugar, spices and vinegar. Generally, chutney is slow-cooked then packed and left to mature for at least 6 weeks so that the flavours are allowed to develop. Chutney eaten before it is ready will taste too strongly of vinegar. Chutneys are ideally served with cold meats or cheese, but can also be used to flavour other recipes.

RELISH contains similar types of ingredients to chutney, but the vegetables are usually more coarsely chopped and the recipes usually contain less vinegar. They are normally ready to eat the day after their preparation, but should be eaten within 2 weeks of opening.

COMMERCIAL FRUIT AND HERB VINEGARS contain fruit and/or herbs that have been steeped in vinegar. I have never enjoyed commercial products much, as I have always found them very harsh and usually with more vinegar than fruit or herb. The method I use in this book produces a delicious variation on the store-bought kind, but it does have a shorter shelf life.

Other methods of preserving

DRYING is an ancient method of preserving. The fruit, vegetables, meat or fish are simply sliced or chopped as necessary and laid out in the sun until dry. They can then be stored without the need for refrigeration and re-hydrated before use. Modern methods include the use of electric desiccators or, in a domestic situation, a low oven.

SALTING, as you might expect, involves leaving vegetables, meat or fish covered in salt until all the moisture has been removed. To use salted food, it must be soaked in several changes of water until re-hydrated, then cooked.

BOTTLING fruit and vegetables usually requires partial cooking, as in tomato sauce, then bottling and heat sealing. The sealed bottles or jars are submerged and boiled for 20 minutes or so, until a vacuum is formed. Bottling requires attention as the glass jars mustn't touch in the water or they will crack. Ingredients must also be carefully chosen. Tomatoes, for example, do not contain sufficient acid to prevent bacterial growth. The solution in this case is the simple addition of a little lemon juice to each bottle.

Selecting fruit and vegetables

SOFT FRUIT AND BERRIES – choose ripe but not soft fruit and pick through thoroughly to remove any mouldy specimens. Overripe fruit will contain too much water to obtain a good set.

CITRUS FRUIT – choose fruit that is heavy for its size, as this will be the juiciest. Make sure the skin is clean and free of marks and blemishes. If you can, choose unwaxed fruit for making marmalade. If you are unable to find any, make sure you scrub the fruit in hot running water using a drop of washing-up liquid. This will remove any wax and insecticide. Dry thoroughly.

VEGETABLES – choose young, fresh vegetables for pickling. If you are making chutney or relish or other preserves that require the vegetables to be chopped, lightly bruised examples can be used as the damage can be removed.

Fruit and vegetables tend to come in gluts at the height of their season. This is the time to buy or harvest, as they will be at their cheapest and best. But just because you have a fridge full of raspberries doesn't mean you have time to preserve them! In this case, it is possible to do part of the preparation and finish off later. For example, cook the fruit for jelly and leave it to strain, then freeze the resulting juice. Thaw, measure and add the sugar when you have time.

Equipment

Although very little specialist equipment is required, a good preserving pan makes the job a little easier. It should be large with a heavy base and made from good quality stainless steel. Some pans also have measurements marked up the inside which, whilst not essential, is certainly helpful both when adding ingredients and when determining the yield of your preserve. A pouring lip is also useful.

The pan will also have sloping sides and a wide top that allows maximum evaporation, essential for reducing the liquid in your preserve to the right concentration. The large size is also important as it allows your ingredients to come to a rolling boil, vital for a good set, without boiling over. Never fill your preserving pan more than halfway.

Jars are, fortunately, re-usable though you may need to replace lids and rubber sealing rings. On the whole, use smaller jars (e.g. 225 g/8 oz) for sweet preserves such as jams, jellies and marmalades, and larger jars (e.g. 500 g/1 lb 2 oz) for pickles, chutneys and other savoury preserves. Most kitchen shops and department stores will stock a selection of jars, though the internet is also a very good source. The jars I used to test the recipes in this book came from a very good eBay shop, for example.

Jam jars will come with metal twist-top lids lined with plastic or rubber, which helps make an airtight seal. You can of course also use waxed discs and cellophane covers for your jam and these are readily available from supermarkets, stationers and good kitchen shops. If in doubt, take a jar with you to make sure you get the correct size.

Wax discs are not suitable for vinegar-based preserves as they do not form an airtight seal and vinegar has a tendency to evaporate. You can use jars with plastic-lined screw tops for these or clip-top jars with rubber seals.

Other essential equipment includes: jelly bag and stand, bowls and basins of varying sizes, small freezer-proof plates, colander, nylon sieve, jam funnel, knives, measuring spoons, thermometer, scales, measuring jugs and spoons, wooden spoons and a good-sized chopping board. You might also find it useful to have a food processor and/or blender to hand. A microwave oven can also come in useful.

Sterilising jars

Properly sterilising your jars, whatever kind you are using, is essential to the process of preserving. All your hard work will be lost if your jam is exposed to any contaminants. It is especially important for jars that have previously contained a vinegar-based preserve so that there is no lingering smell to spoil the next batch.

If you are re-using old jars, first check for cracks or chips. Wash all jars thoroughly in hot soapy water, removing any old labels at this stage. Rinse the jars in freshly boiled water then turn upside down on a clean tea towel or kitchen paper to drain.

There are two main methods for heat sterilising your jars at this stage. For the first: preheat the oven to Gas Mark 3/170°C/325°F. Stand the jars on a baking sheet, trying to avoid them touching, and heat in the oven for 10 minutes. Remove from the oven and either fill hot with hot preserves or leave until cold to fill with cold mixtures. For the second: put the clean jars in a deep pan and cover with boiling water. Bring to the boil and boil for 10 minutes. Remove carefully (there are specialist tongs available for this purpose), drain well and fill whilst hot with hot preserves or leave until cold to fill with cold mixtures.

It is also possible to sterilise jars in the microwave – please check the manufacturer's instructions for your model. As a general guide, half-fill clean jars with fresh water and microwave on full power until the water boils. Use oven gloves to remove the jars from the microwave and swirl the water around inside them. Discard the water then stand the jars upside down on a clean tea towel or kitchen paper. Use the jar as described above.

Preparing fruit and vegetables

BERRIES AND OTHER SOFT FRUIT: Berries need little preparation, but do check over the fruit to make sure that none of it is soft or mouldy. Remove any stray leaves and stems and rinse thoroughly in a colander then drain well, drying on kitchen paper if necessary. For strawberries, pinch out the calyx, giving a slight twist to remove the little white core too. To remove redcurrants and white currants from their stems, hold the top of the bunch over a bowl then insert a fork above the top cluster of berries. At the same time, push down on the fork and pull up on the stem – the berries will pop off easily.

CITRUS FRUIT: A medium-size sharp knife is essential to cut citrus peel into the thin shreds needed for marmalade, but you can also use scissors or even the slicing disc of a food processor (the result will not be as neat, but this is not always the most important thing).

🍃 You'll get more juice from your citrus fruit if you warm it gently first – pop whole fruit into the microwave and heat on full power for 15–30 seconds, depending on size. Rolling the fruit gently on the work surface before cutting in half also helps extract the maximum juice.

Sugar

A trip to your local supermarket will reveal shelves groaning with different types of sugar. Which to use? First, be guided by your recipe, which should always specify what to use, but if it doesn't, here are some tips.

In the UK, some of the sugar we use is from sugar beet grown in the UK, and the remainder is from sugar cane grown in warmer climates, such as the Caribbean and Mauritius. The most obvious difference between types of sugar is colour. When sugar is

extracted from both beet and cane, it becomes a strongly flavoured black syrup (molasses). White sugar has had all of the molasses removed. Brown sugars vary in darkness and stickiness depending on the amount of molasses remaining.

In addition, sugars differ according to the fineness of the crystals. Caster sugar is very fine and is most often used in baking, as it is easily incorporated, for example into butter for a sponge cake. I like to use it in preserves, as I find it dissolves quickly. Granulated sugar is coarser than caster sugar and is quite popular for stirring into hot drinks. As it is less refined, it is also cheaper than caster sugar. I think it is interchangeable with caster sugar in preserves. You will also see golden granulated and golden caster sugars on the shelves. These have the same consistency as white caster and granulated sugar, but retain some molasses. For this reason, they also have a slightly stronger flavour. They are a little more expensive too.

Preserving sugar is a very large crystal white sugar. It dissolves more slowly and does not settle on the bottom of the pan, reducing the risk of burning. It may also reduce the need for stirring and skimming. It is, however, the most expensive of white sugars.

Jam sugar contains added pectin, making it ideal for use with low-pectin fruits. It is a similar price to caster sugar.

Skinning peaches, nectarines and tomatoes

Choose ripe fruit that is firm but not soft. It should also have a strong fragrance. Cut a small cross in the skin on the base of the fruit using a sharp knife. Put the fruit into a large deep bowl then pour over freshly boiled water. Leave for no longer than 1 minute (less if you can see the skin pulling away from the flesh), then drain and rinse under cold water. Leave until cool enough to handle – the skin will pull away easily, especially at the point where you cut the little cross.

Useful tips

JELLIES: When getting ready to strain your mixture for jelly, scald the bag first so that the juice will run through and not be absorbed by the fabric. Allow enough time for the juice to drip through on its own – plan to start one day and finish the next. If you try to hurry the process and squeeze the bag, you may end up with a cloudy jelly.

MARMALADE: The fruit and juice mixture needs to reduce by about half before you add the sugar. You may find it useful to cover the mixture for the first 1–1½ hours to get the peel really soft without losing too much volume, then cook for 1 hour more, uncovered, until reduced by half. This will ensure that the mixture is the right concentration for a good set.

Make sure the peel is completely soft – test by removing a bit of peel and allow it to cool briefly. It should squash easily in your fingers. If you're using more than one type of citrus in a single recipe, test all the fruit, as the time they need to become soft varies.

Adding sugar to jams, jellies and marmalades

If you find that the sugar takes a long time to thoroughly dissolve, try warming it first, either in a low oven for 10 minutes or so, or in the microwave on full power for 1 minute. It's important to learn to recognize the right moment to add the sugar. As a rule of thumb, slow cooking before the sugar is added then rapid and short cooking afterwards.

What makes a good set?

Jams, jellies and marmalades all rely on the right combination of pectin, acid and sugar to achieve a good set. Fruit contains varying amounts of pectin and acid – in fact, the same type of fruit may contain different quantities of acid and pectin from year to year or variety to variety. Look to your recipe for guidance.

Acid helps in the process of extracting the pectin from the fruit. It is essential for a good set and helps prevent crystallization of the sugar. Fruit that is rich in pectin is usually rich in acid too. There are fruits that require the addition of extra acid in the form of lemon juice, redcurrant or apple stock. Again, your recipe should offer guidance.

High pectin fruit includes blackcurrants, redcurrants, damsons, quinces, cooking apples, gooseberries and cranberries. Medium pectin fruit includes raspberries, early blackberries, apricots, greengages, and loganberries. Low pectin fruit includes strawberries, pears, elderberries, cherries and late blackberries.

Sugar is not just for sweetness. The concentration of sugar in the final preserve will determine whether it will keep well or not or whether the preserve will ferment or crystallize. The explanation for this is a complex chemical one, beyond the remit of this introduction. A good recipe should remove the need to understand the process!

Pectin is found in the cell walls of all plant food. It is a natural gum-like substance. Pectin is most easily extracted from just ripe and slightly under-ripe fruit. The pectin from overripe fruit will not gel. You don't usually need to measure the pectin content of your fruit if you are using a reliable recipe. If you are using low pectin fruit it is often blended with a high pectin fruit – or commercial pectin may be called for.

Testing for a set – jams, jellies and marmalades

There are three main tests for determining whether your sweet preserve has reached setting point. Take the preserve off the heat during testing in order to ensure that it doesn't overcook.

FLAKE TEST: Dip a clean wooden spoon into the mixture in the pan. Remove it and, holding it above the pan, twirl the spoon a few times to cool the mixture slightly. Allow the mixture to fall off the spoon. If the drops run together and form flakes that hang on the edge of the spoon, setting point is reached.

COLD SAUCER TEST: Chill a couple of small plates in the refrigerator or freezer. Put a small blob of the mixture on to the cold plate and tilt to spread it thinly. Leave to cool for a minute, then push the mixture with your finger; if it wrinkles, it's reached setting point.

THERMOMETER TEST: Stir the mixture in the pan. Dip the thermometer into hot water before adding it to the pan. If the temperature reaches 105°C/220°F, setting point should have been reached. Double-check using the saucer test to be certain.

Testing for a set – chutney

To test whether your chutney is ready, use a wooden spoon to drag a channel through the mixture, exposing the bottom of the pan. If the channel immediately fills with liquid, your chutney is not yet ready. If the channel does not fill and the bottom of the pan remains visible, the chutney is ready for bottling and should be removed from the heat.

Extracting pectin for marmalade

When you are making marmalade, the recipe will usually instruct you to place all the membranes and pips from the citrus fruit on to a large square of muslin. This is because a lot of the pectin is contained in the membranes and pips but you don't want them

in your finished marmalade. You then draw the muslin into a small, not too tightly bound, bag which you suspend in the contents of the pan. Leave a long bit of string to tie the bag to the handle of the pan as this will make it easy to remove later. Once the peel is fully cooked, remove this bag and squeeze it to remove the pectin, which you add to the pan.

Muslin is available from good kitchen shops, either sold off the roll or in measured squares or bags. It is inexpensive and is a very useful kitchen aid. It can be washed and re-used many times.

Potting

Once you have determined that your mixture has reached setting point, you are ready to pot. Make sure you are prepared and that your jars and lids are clean and sterilised. You may find it helpful to organize a kind of production line, with everything lined up in a convenient and safe way.

First, remove any froth or scum that has formed on the surface of your preserve. It isn't harmful but it isn't attractive and often sets more firmly than the rest of the preserve, giving you little lumps in the jar. Wait until the jam has reached setting point before removing it from the heat and then either adding a little knob of butter and stirring (which will often deal with all of the froth) or simply using a metal spoon to skim it off.

I prefer to put hot jam into hot jars but this has obvious disadvantages as it can be dangerous. I line up my hot jars on the baking sheet they sat on in the oven and then I use a non-stick jam funnel (this means I don't have to touch the jar). I then use a kitchen ladle to spoon the jam in up to the rim – it's important to fill the jars right up to prevent any airborne bacteria getting a foothold. The filling will shrink as it cools and form a good vacuum seal. Fill all the jars this way. I then add the screw-top lid and tighten it lightly before lifting the jar using an oven-glove, then tightening firmly. Set the filled jars aside until cold.

Label your jars once they are cold (sticky labels may come off if applied to hot jars). Put both the name of the preserve and the date on which it was bottled – you might also make note of the recipe source. I find it quite straightforward to make colourful labels using my computer and some clipart, but most stationers sell matching labels and decorative covers, which you may prefer. Use scraps of wrapping paper or pretty fabric to make tops for your preserves if you are planning to give them as gifts. Preserves decorated in this way make good contributions to children's school fêtes or WI markets.

Storage

Most preserves, if made using a reliable recipe that contains the right proportion of sugar, salt or vinegar as appropriate, will keep for up to a year – and some will certainly keep for longer, given the right storage conditions. Preserves like to be kept in cool, dry, dark conditions. The contents will shrink if conditions are too hot, dampness may cause mould to form and bright conditions may cause the contents to fade. I keep my preserves in the cupboard under the stairs, as it seems to meet most of these conditions fairly well, being unheated, unlit and reasonably dry. A dry shed or garage might be an alternative.

Once opened, all preserves are subject to contamination by airborne bacteria and should be consumed within a few weeks. Keep opened jars in the fridge.

Exceptions to these storage times include fruit curds which, because they contain butter and eggs, will only keep, heat-sealed as described above, for about 6 weeks. Once opened, they should be eaten within 2 weeks.

Low sugar jams and fruit compôtes should be stored, heat-sealed as described above, for about 6 months only. Once opened, use the jam or compôte within 2 weeks.

Jams and Conserves

What better way to take advantage of a glut of soft, summer fruit than to make a delicious and colourful jam or conserve? And don't think jam is just for soft fruit, because a wide range of fruit can be used to great effect. The terms 'jam' and 'conserve' are often used interchangeably, but here I have used 'conserve' to denote recipes that also contain nuts and/or dried fruits.

In this chapter you'll find recipes for traditional favourites as well as fresh and dried apricots, blueberries, gooseberries, rhubarb, figs, apples and even the unprepossessing marrow. This selection should enable you to make preserves all year round.

Strawberry Jam

Makes: *6 x 225 ml (8 fl oz) jars*
Preparation & cooking time: *25 minutes*

The classic, must-have jam. It's worth a trip to the local pick-your-own just to have some in the cupboard.

1 kg (2 lb 4 oz) strawberries, hulled and wiped
juice of 1 large lemon
1 kg (2 lb 4 oz) granulated sugar

1 Put the strawberries into a large pan or preserving pan with the lemon juice. Bring to a simmer, just until the juices begin to run – about 10 minutes.

2 Carefully mash the strawberries with a potato masher and simmer for a further 5 minutes until you have a thick purée.

3 Add the sugar and stir gently until completely dissolved. Return the mixture to a rolling boil and boil for 5 minutes before removing any scum. Test for a set (page 12) and, if necessary, boil for a minute more, then test again. Continue testing at 1-minute intervals until the jam has reached setting point.

4 Remove from the heat, skim off any scum, and allow the jam to cool briefly before carefully pouring into sterilised jars (page 9). Allow the jam to cool completely before labelling and storing.

Raspberry or Blackberry Jam

Using 1 kg (2 lb 4 oz) raspberries or blackberries and 1 kg (2 lb 4 oz) granulated sugar, follow the method for Strawberry Jam (page 16). There is no need to mash the fruit at stage 2.

Blackcurrant Jam

Using 1 kg (2 lb 4 oz) blackcurrants and 1.3 kg (2 lb 12 oz) granulated sugar and omitting the lemon juice, follow the method for Strawberry Jam (page 16), but without mashing the fruit at stage 2. Allow the jam to simmer for just 3 minutes once the sugar has dissolved, before testing for a set.

Cherry and Redcurrant Jam

Using 1 kg (2 lb 4 oz) cherries (weight before stoning), 500 g (1 lb 2 oz) redcurrants and 1.5 kg (3 lb 5 oz) granulated sugar, follow the method for Strawberry Jam (page 16), omitting the lemon juice but adding 150 ml (¼ pint) water. When the sugar has dissolved, simmer the fruit for about 30 minutes before testing for a set.

Strawberry Freezer Jam

Makes: *7 x 225 ml (8 fl oz) jars*
Preparation & cooking time: *2 hours + 2–3 hours standing*

Although this jam doesn't have a firm, traditional set, like a cooked jam, the fresh, fruity flavour more than makes up for it. My mother used to make this jam when I was a child and now I make it with my children, as it is quite safe for them to help.

650 g (1 lb 7 oz) strawberries
1.25 kg (3 lb) caster sugar
3 tablespoons lemon juice
½ x 250 ml (9 fl oz) bottle liquid pectin

1 Mash the strawberries in a large bowl until quite juicy – leave it chunky or mash more thoroughly if you prefer a smoother jam. Add the sugar and stir at regular intervals until completely dissolved (this may take an hour or more).

2 Stir in the lemon juice and liquid pectin and continue to stir for 2 minutes. Ladle into small freezer-proof containers and leave to stand in a warm kitchen for 2–3 hours. Check after this time to see if the jam is beginning to set. If the set appears very thin, i.e. still quite liquid, pour the jam back into the bowl and add another tablespoon of lemon juice and repeat.

3 Leave for 24 hours at room temperature before labelling and freezing. Keep for up to 6 months. Allow the jam to thaw completely in the refrigerator before using.

Raspberry Freezer Jam

Replace the strawberries with raspberries, but use only 2 tablespoons of lemon juice because raspberries are more acidic than strawberries.

Microwave Jam

Makes: *3 x 225 ml (8 fl oz) jars*
Preparation & cooking time: *25 minutes*

Because this jam has to be made in a measuring jug, it makes a relatively small quantity.

500 g (1 lb 2 oz) strawberries, raspberries, blackberries or other berries (or a mixture)
3 tablespoons lemon juice
500 g (1 lb 2 oz) golden caster sugar

1 Wash and hull the strawberries and place in a large microwaveable measuring jug with the lemon juice.

2 Cook on full power for about 4 minutes or until the fruit is soft – the time this takes will vary according to the power of your microwave. (The time given is for an 800W or E rated microwave). Stir in the sugar and allow to dissolve completely. Cook, stirring every 3 minutes and removing any scum as it forms, until the jam sets when a little is placed on a chilled saucer. This will take about 16–20 minutes.

3 Leave the jam to stand for 5 minutes before pouring into hot sterilised jars (page 9). Seal tightly and allow the jam to cool completely before labelling and storing.

Blueberry and Lemon Jam

Makes: *2 x 225 ml (8 fl oz) jars*
Preparation & cooking time: *30 minutes*

This jam has a delightful fragrance from the unusual addition of bay. If you happen across wild blueberries, use them instead for an even more intense fruit flavour.

500 g (1 lb 2 oz) blueberries
4 tablespoons lemon juice plus zest of 1 lemon
1 fresh bay leaf
500 g (1 lb 2 oz) granulated sugar

1 Put the blueberries, lemon juice and zest and bay leaf into a large pan or preserving pan. Simmer for 10 minutes until the juices begin to run. Remove the bay leaf.

2 Add the sugar and stir over a low heat until dissolved. Increase the heat and boil for about 15 minutes before testing for a set (page 12). If necessary boil for a further 1 minute, then test again. Continue testing at 1-minute intervals, as necessary, until the jam has reached setting point.

3 Remove the pan from the heat, skim off any scum, and allow the jam to cool briefly before carefully pouring into hot sterilised jars (page 9). Seal the jars and allow the jam to cool completely before labelling and storing.

Spiced Dried Apricot Jam

Makes: *6 x 225 ml (8 fl oz) jars*
Preparation & cooking time: *2½ hours + soaking overnight*

If you prefer to use dried, non-sulphured apricots for this jam, follow the instructions on the packet for re-hydrating. The flavour will be the same, but the colour will be less vibrant.

500 g (1 lb 2 oz) ready-to-eat dried apricots, roughly chopped
1 vanilla pod, split lengthwise
1 cinnamon stick
1 star anise
2 strips lemon zest
juice of 1 lemon
1.2 litres (2 pints) water
1 kg (2 lb 4 oz) soft brown sugar

1 Cover the apricots with water by about 2.5 cm (1 inch) and leave overnight.

2 Next day, tie the vanilla pod, cinnamon stick, star anise and lemon zest together with a piece of kitchen string, or wrap in a small piece of muslin and tie shut.

3 Drain the apricots well and put into a large pan or preserving pan with the measured water. Bring to the boil and simmer for about 45 minutes to 1 hour until soft.

4 Add the spice bundle, lemon juice and sugar. Stir well over a low heat until the sugar has dissolved. Bring to a simmer and cook for 1¼–1½ hours before testing for a set (page 12). Boil for a further 5 minutes, if necessary, then test again. Continue testing at 5-minute intervals, as necessary, until the jam has reached setting point.

5 Remove the pan from the heat, take out the spice bundle, skim off any scum and allow the jam to cool briefly before carefully pouring into hot sterilised jars (page 9). Seal and label the jars then allow the jam to cool completely before storing.

Raspberry and Lime Jam

Makes: *6 x 225 ml (8 fl oz) jars*
Preparation & cooking time: *25 minutes*

The addition of lime makes this one of the most interesting jams in the book and a personal favourite.

1 kg (2 lb 4 oz) raspberries
juice and zest of 2 large limes
1 kg (2 lb 4 oz) granulated sugar

1 Put the fruit into a large pan or preserving pan with the lime juice and zest. Bring to a simmer just until the juices begin to run – about 5–7 minutes.

2 Add the sugar and stir gently until completely dissolved. Return the mixture to a rolling boil and boil for 5 minutes before removing any scum. Test for a set (page 12) and, if necessary, boil for a further minute, then test again. Continue testing at 1-minute intervals, as necessary, until the jam has reached setting point.

3 Remove from the heat, skim off any scum, and allow the jam to cool slightly before carefully pouring into hot sterilised jars (page 9). Seal the jars and allow the jam to cool completely before labelling and storing.

Gooseberry and Elderflower Jam

Makes: *6 x 225 ml (8 fl oz) jars*
Preparation & cooking time: *30 minutes*

A classic combination, this version uses elderflower cordial – in case you don't have any access to fresh elderflowers.

**1 kg (2 lb 4 oz) gooseberries, topped
  and tailed**
1 kg (2 lb 4 oz) granulated sugar
4 tablespoons elderflower cordial

1 Put the gooseberries into a large pan or preserving pan along with 150 ml (¼ pint) water. Bring to the boil and simmer for about 10 minutes until the fruit is soft.

2 Add the sugar and stir over a low heat until completely dissolved. Increase the heat and boil for about 8 minutes before testing for a set (page 12). If necessary, boil for another minute then test again. Continue testing at 1-minute intervals, as necessary, until the jam has reached setting point.

3 Remove the pan from the heat, skim off any scum, and allow the jam to cool briefly then stir in the elderflower cordial. Carefully pour into hot sterilised jars (page 9). Seal the jars and allow the jam to cool completely before labelling and storing.

Damson Jam

Makes: *7 x 225 ml (8 fl oz) jars*
Preparation & cooking time: *45 minutes*

Damsons make excellent jam as they break down well and produce a luscious dark-coloured preserve that is full of flavour.

1.25 kg (2 lb 12 oz) damsons
500 ml (18 fl oz) water
1.5 kg (3 lb 5 oz) sugar

1 Remove the stalks, wash the damsons and put into a large pan or preserving pan with the water. Cook slowly for about 30 minutes until the damsons have broken down.

2 Add the sugar and stir over a low heat until dissolved. Increase the heat and boil for about 10 minutes before testing for a set (page 12). Remove the stones as they rise to the surface, allowing any liquid to drip back into the pan. If necessary, boil for another minute then test again. Continue testing at 1-minute intervals, as necessary, until the jam has reached setting point.

3 Remove from the heat, skim off any scum, and allow the jam to cool briefly before carefully pouring into hot sterilised jars (page 9). Seal the jars and allow the jam to cool completely before labelling and storing.

Blackberry and Apple Jam

Makes: *8 x 225 ml (8 fl oz) jars*
Preparation & cooking time: *1 hour 20 minutes*

This is such a fantastic combination in crumbles that I thought why not? The apple gives the jam a good set too.

375 g (13 oz) cooking apples, peeled and roughly chopped
360 ml (12 fl oz) water
1 kg (2 lb 4 oz) blackberries
1.25 kg (3 lb) granulated sugar

1 Put the apples and water into a large saucepan or preserving pan, bring to the boil then reduce the heat and simmer for about 20–30 minutes until soft.

2 Add the blackberries, together with the sugar, and cook over a low heat, stirring constantly, until the sugar has dissolved. Increase the heat and boil for 30 minutes before testing for a set (page 12). If necessary, boil for a further 5 minutes then test again. Continue testing at 1-minute intervals, as necessary, until the jam has reached setting point.

3 Remove from the heat, skim off any scum, and allow the jam to cool briefly before carefully pouring into hot sterilised jars (page 9). Seal the jars and allow the jam to cool completely before labelling and storing.

Marrow and Ginger Jam

Makes: *6 x 225 ml (8 fl oz) jars*
Preparation & cooking time: *1 hour + macerating overnight*

1 kg (2 lb 4 oz) marrow, peeled, de-seeded and diced into 1 cm (½ inch) cubes
1 kg (2 lb 4 oz) preserving sugar
juice and zest of 2 lemons
50 g (2 oz) fresh ginger, roughly chopped

1 Put the prepared marrow into a large bowl along with the sugar. Cover and leave in the refrigerator overnight.

2 The following day, transfer the marrow and sugar to a large pan or preserving pan along with the lemon juice and zest. Bash the ginger with a rolling pin and place in a muslin bag. Add to the pan.

3 Bring to the boil and simmer for about 45 minutes before testing for a set (page 12). If necessary, boil for a further 5 minutes then test again. Continue testing at 5-minute intervals, as necessary, until the jam has reached setting point.

4 Remove the muslin bag, skim off any scum, and allow the jam to cool briefly. Carefully pour into hot sterilised jars (page 9). Seal the jars and allow the jam to cool completely before labelling and storing.

Caramelised Apple Jam

Makes: *10 x 225 ml (8 fl oz) jars*
Preparation & cooking time: *1 hour*

This recipe makes use of commercially available bottled caramel. If you are unable to find any, make a dark caramel by heating 150 g (5 oz) caster sugar. When the caramel is a dark golden colour, remove from the heat and add 3 tablespoons of water, being careful to avoid the hot spitting sugar. Stir over a low heat until smooth then add a bit more water to get a thick syrup and use this instead.

2 kg (4 lb 8 oz) cooking apples
1.2 litres (2 pints) water
juice of 2 lemons
1.8 kg (4 lb) granulated sugar
150 ml (¼ pint) ready-made caramel

1 Peel and core the apples, reserving the peel and core and tying into a small muslin bag. Roughly chop the apples before placing into a large pan or preserving pan along with the water and muslin bag. Simmer for about 20 minutes until completely soft. Remove the muslin bag and, if necessary, mash the apple flesh with a potato masher until smooth.

2 Add the lemon juice and sugar and stir over a low heat until the sugar has completely dissolved. Increase the heat and return to a boil. Cook for about 30 minutes before testing for a set (page 12). If necessary, boil for another minute then test again. Continue testing at 1-minute intervals, as necessary, until the jam has reached setting point.

3 Remove the pan from the heat, skim off any scum, and allow the jam to cool briefly before adding the caramel and stirring thoroughly. Carefully pour the jam into hot sterilised jars (page 9). Seal the jars and allow the jam to cool completely before labelling and storing.

Fig Jam

Makes: *2 x 225 ml (8 fl oz) jars*
Preparation & cooking time: *40 minutes +
2 hours macerating*

**1 kg (2 lb 4 oz) fresh figs, stems removed and
flesh roughly chopped**
750 g (1 lb 10 oz) caster sugar
1 tablespoon ground allspice
1 teaspoon ground cinnamon
juice and zest of ½ lemon

1 Weigh the figs again after trimming and
chopping. If necessary, reduce the amount
of sugar proportionately or add another fig to
increase the weight. Transfer to a large bowl
along with the sugar. Add the spices, lemon
juice and zest. Cover with a clean tea towel
and leave to stand for about 2 hours, stirring
occasionally.

2 Transfer the mixture to a large pan or
preserving pan. Slowly bring the mixture to
the boil, stirring regularly until the sugar has
dissolved. Increase the heat and boil gently
for 30 minutes before testing for a set (page
12). If necessary, boil for a further 5 minutes
then test again. Continue testing at 5-minute
intervals, as necessary, until the jam has
reached setting point.

3 Remove the pan from the heat, skim off
any scum and allow the jam to cool briefly.
Carefully pour into hot sterilised jars (page
9). Seal the jars and allow the jam to cool
completely before labelling and storing.

Rhubarb and Ginger Jam

Makes: *4 x 225 ml (8 fl oz) jars*
Preparation & cooking time: *40 minutes +
overnight macerating*

1 kg (2 lb 4 oz) rhubarb
1 kg (2 lb 4 oz) granulated sugar
**50 g (2 oz) preserved ginger (page 116),
drained and finely chopped**
juice of 1 lemon

1 Trim, wash and wipe the rhubarb and cut into
2.5 cm (1 inch) pieces. Put into a large bowl,
toss with the sugar, cover with a clean tea
towel and leave overnight.

2 Next day, pour the rhubarb mixture into a large
pan or preserving pan (most of the sugar will
have dissolved) and add the preserved ginger
and lemon juice. Bring slowly to the boil,
stirring occasionally, until any remaining sugar
has dissolved.

3 Boil rapidly for about 30 minutes before
testing for a set (page 12). If necessary, boil for
a further 5 minutes then test again. Continue
testing at 5-minute intervals, as necessary,
until the jam has reached setting point.

4 Remove the pan from the heat, skim off
any scum and allow the jam to cool briefly.
Carefully pour the jam into hot sterilised jars
(page 9). Seal the jars and allow the jam to
cool completely before labelling and storing.

Rhubarb Vanilla Jam

Makes: *5 x 225 ml (8 fl oz) jars*
Preparation & cooking time: *45 minutes + overnight macerating*

Try to use early forced rhubarb for jam – the bright pink stuff.
It's less watery and much sweeter than its late-season cousin,
which produces a kind of sludgy-green jam.

1 kg (2 lb 4 oz) rhubarb
1 kg (2 lb 4 oz) granulated sugar
1 vanilla pod, split lengthwise
juice of 1 lemon

1 Trim, wash and wipe the rhubarb and cut into 2.5 cm (1 inch) pieces. Put into a large bowl, toss with the sugar, cover with a clean tea towel and leave overnight.

2 Next day, pour the rhubarb mixture into a large pan or preserving pan (most of the sugar will have dissolved) and add the vanilla pod and the lemon juice. Bring slowly to the boil, stirring occasionally, until any remaining sugar has dissolved.

3 Boil rapidly for about 1–1¼ hours, until darkened and thickened, before testing for a set (page 12). If necessary, boil for a further 5 minutes, then test again. Continue testing at 5–minute intervals, as necessary, until the jam has reached setting point.

4 Remove from the heat, skim off any scum, and allow to cool briefly. Carefully pour the jam into hot sterilised jars (page 9). Seal and allow to cool completely before labelling and storing.

Apricot and Ginger Conserve

Makes: *5 x 225 ml (8 fl oz) jars*
Preparation & cooking time: *30 minutes*

This is my favourite recipe in the book. The apricots lend a subtle sharpness and the chunks of ginger are always a little surprise in the mouth. Try this one … go on.

1 kg (2 lb 4 oz) fresh apricots
1 kg (2 lb 4 oz) granulated sugar
150 ml (¼ pint) water
50 g (2 oz) crystallized ginger, roughly chopped

1 Halve and stone the apricots, reserving about half the stones. Roughly chop the flesh.

2 Crack the stones, exposing the kernel inside, and place in a piece of muslin. Tie into a bag.

3 Put the apricots, sugar, water and muslin bag into a large pan or preserving pan. Bring slowly to the boil, stirring often, until all the sugar has dissolved. Add the ginger and increase the heat. Bring the mixture to a rolling boil and cook for about 20 minutes before testing for a set (page 12). If necessary, boil for a further minute then test again. Continue testing at 1-minute intervals, as necessary, until the jam has reached setting point.

4 Remove from the heat, take out the muslin bag, skim off any scum, and allow the mixture to cool briefly. Carefully pour the conserve into hot sterilised jars (page 9). Seal the jars and allow the conserve to cool completely before labelling and storing.

Peach and Almond Conserve

Makes: *2 x 225 ml (8 fl oz) jars*
Preparation & cooking time: *30 minutes + 1 hour macerating*

Peaches and almonds are a classic combination. Using brown sugar gives this jam a very rich, dark body with chunks of peach. It has a softer set than jam so is suitable for serving with vanilla ice cream, for example.

1.5 kg (3 lb 5oz) ripe but firm peaches, peeled and sliced
750 g (1lb 10 oz) light brown soft sugar
juice and zest of 1 lemon
200 g (7 oz) raisins
100 g (3½ oz) blanched almonds, roughly chopped

1 Put the sliced peaches, sugar and lemon into a large bowl. Toss together well and cover with a clean tea towel. Leave to stand for 1 hour, by which time most of the sugar will have dissolved. Transfer to a large pan or preserving pan and cook gently, stirring often, until all the sugar has dissolved.

2 Increase the heat and bring to the boil. Cook for 20 minutes before adding the raisins and almonds. Simmer for a further 5 minutes before testing for a set (page 12). If necessary, boil for another minute then test again. Continue testing at 1-minute intervals, as necessary, until the jam has reached setting point.

3 Remove the pan from the heat, skim off any scum, and allow the jam to cool briefly. Carefully pour into hot sterilised jars (page 9). Seal the jars and allow the jam to cool completely before labelling and storing.

Peach, Raisin, Pecan and Rum Conserve

Makes: *7 x 225 ml (8 fl oz) jars*
Preparation & cooking time: *45 minutes + 1 hour macerating*

This is a brightly coloured jam full of dried fruit and nuts. The rum gives it a really exotic taste, which is difficult to place at first.

1.5 kg (3 lb 5 oz) peaches, peeled and cut
   into slices
750 g (1 lb 10 oz) caster sugar
juice and zest of 1 lemon
150 g (5 oz) raisins
100 g (3½ oz) pecans, roughly chopped
75 ml (3 fl oz) dark rum

1 Put the sliced peaches, sugar and lemon into a large bowl. Cover with a clean tea towel and leave to stand for 1 hour. Transfer to a large pan or preserving pan and cook gently, stirring often, until all the sugar has dissolved.

2 Bring to the boil and cook for 20 minutes before adding the raisins and pecans. Simmer for a further 5 minutes before testing for a set (page 12). If necessary, boil for another minute then test again. Continue testing at 1-minute intervals, as necessary, until the jam has reached setting point.

3 Remove from the heat, skim off any scum and allow the jam to cool briefly before stirring in the rum. Carefully pour the mixture into hot sterilised jars (page 9). Seal the jars and allow the jam to cool completely before labelling and storing.

Cinnamon and Raisin Apple Conserve

Makes: *7 x 225 ml (8 fl oz) jars*
Preparation & cooking time: *45 minutes*

I first had a jam such as this in Normandy, famous for its apples and apple products. It is absolutely divine spread on a toasted, buttered crumpet.

1.5 kg (3 lb 5 oz) unpeeled Bramley apples, finely chopped (weighed after chopping)
150 ml (¼ pint) water
3 tablespoons lemon juice
75 g (3 oz) raisins
1 kg (2 lb 4 oz) granulated sugar
1 teaspoon ground cinnamon

1 Put the chopped apples, water, lemon juice and raisins into a large pan or preserving pan. Bring to the boil over a high heat. Add the sugar and cinnamon and bring to the boil, stirring constantly.

2 Boil rapidly for 5 minutes. Test for a set (page 12). If necessary boil for another minute, then test again. Continue testing at 1–minute intervals, as necessary, until the jam has reached setting point.

3 Remove from the heat, skim off any scum, and allow the jam to cool for about 20 minutes. Carefully pour into hot sterilised jars (page 9). Seal the jars and allow to cool completely before labelling and storing.

Strawberry, Raspberry and Hazelnut Conserve

Makes: *6 x 225 ml (8 fl oz) jars*
Preparation & cooking time: *: 25 minutes + macerating for 3 days*

The whole fruits make this conserve quite spectacular, though it doesn't set as firmly as jam. Use it to sandwich a Victoria sponge along with fresh, softly whipped double cream.

500 g (1 lb 2 oz) strawberries, hulled and wiped
500 g (1 lb 2 oz) raspberries
1 kg (2 lb 4 oz) granulated sugar
juice of 1 large lemon
75 g (3 oz) toasted hazelnuts, roughly chopped

1 Put the whole fruits into a large bowl, layered with the sugar. Cover with a clean tea towel and leave overnight.

2 Transfer the fruit and sugar mixture to a large pan or preserving pan and add the lemon juice. Bring to the boil, stirring often until the sugar has completely dissolved. Cook for 5 minutes, stirring occasionally.

3 Return the mixture to the bowl, cover with a cloth and leave for a further 48 hours.

4 Return the mixture to the large pan, bring back to the boil and cook for 10 minutes, stirring occasionally. Add the hazelnuts and cook for a further minute before testing for a set (page 12). If necessary, boil for another minute then test again. Continue testing at 1-minute intervals, as necessary, until the jam has reached setting point.

5 Remove the pan from the heat, skim off any scum and allow the mixture to cool briefly. Carefully pour the mixture into hot sterilised jars (page 9). Seal the jars and allow the conserve to cool completely before labelling and storing.

Jellies

Jellies are less popular in the UK than they are in America (the ubiquitous 'peanut butter and jelly' sandwich being testament to this), but we do have our popular favourites, including rosehip, crab apple, redcurrant and, of course, mint jelly. Jellies are very straightforward to make, though the task is made easier still by a little specialist equipment. I bought a fantastic jelly strainer that adjusts to the size of your bowl and holds the jelly bag suspended safely. Try the Cranberry and Port Jelly at Christmas with your turkey (and especially afterwards, in your turkey sandwiches). And, if you come across some flavourful grapes, why not give Grape Jelly a go? 'PB&J' may yet catch on.

Redcurrant Jelly

Makes: *2 x 225 ml (8 fl oz) jars*
Preparation & cooking time: *45 minutes + straining overnight*

Easy to make and probably the most useful preserve to have in the kitchen, redcurrant jelly is fabulous with just about any cold meat. Try it with roast venison too.

1 kg (2 lb 4 oz) redcurrants
1 litre (1¾ pints) water
caster sugar (see step 3 for quantity)

1 Place the washed fruit – stalks and all – in a large pan or preserving pan with the water and bring slowly to the boil. Simmer for about 30 minutes, stirring and mashing the fruit well.

2 Strain through a jelly bag or muslin-lined nylon sieve, set over a large bowl. Don't be tempted to press the fruit or squeeze the bag, as this will cause the jelly to become cloudy. Leave until the dripping has stopped. This may take several hours or even overnight.

3 When the dripping has stopped, discard the solids in the jelly bag and carefully measure the resulting liquid. Return it to the preserving pan along with 450 g (1 lb) caster sugar for each 600 ml (1 pint) of liquid. Stir well over a low heat until the sugar has dissolved completely.

4 Increase the heat and boil rapidly for 10–15 minutes before testing for a set (page 12). If necessary, boil for a further minute then test again. Continue testing at 1-minute intervals, as necessary, until the jelly has reached setting point.

5 Remove the pan from the heat, skim off any scum and allow the jelly to cool briefly. Carefully pour the jelly into hot sterilised jars (page 9). Seal the jars and allow the jelly to cool completely before labelling and storing.

Blackcurrant Jelly

Follow the instructions for redcurrant jelly, using the same weight of fruit and the same proportion of sugar to strained juice.

Grape Jelly

Weigh out 1 kg (2 lb 4 oz) flavourful grapes, such as Muscat, preferably with seeds. Barely cover the grapes with water in a large pan or preserving pan. Add the juice of 1 lemon and simmer for about 30 minutes until soft. Use a potato masher to extract as much juice as possible. Strain as above (step 2). Leave the mixture until the dripping has stopped (up to 12 hours). Measure the juice and use 450 g (1 lb) caster sugar for each 600 ml (1 pint) of liquid. Continue from step 4 above.

Blackberry Jelly

Follow the recipe for redcurrant jelly, replacing the redcurrants with blackberries and adding 4 tablespoons of lemon juice during the initial cooking. Add caster sugar in the same proportion as for redcurrant jelly and continue from step 4.

Cherry Jelly

Follow the recipe for redcurrant jelly, replacing the redcurrants with red or black cherries (no need to stone) and adding 4 tablespoons of lemon juice during the initial cooking. Add caster sugar, as for redcurrant jelly, and half a 250 ml (9 fl oz) bottle of liquid pectin. Stir well, simmer for 1 minute then continue from step 4.

Crab Apple Jelly

Makes: *2 x 225 ml (8 fl oz) jars*
Preparation & cooking time: *45 minutes + straining overnight*

1 kg (2 lb 4 oz) crab apples
juice of 1 lemon
caster sugar (see step 3 for quantity)

1 Wash and pick over the apples to remove stems and leaves. Put them into a large pan or preserving pan and just cover with water. Bring to the boil and simmer for about 30 minutes until the fruit is very soft. Mash well.

2 Strain through a jelly bag or muslin-lined nylon sieve, set over a large bowl. Don't be tempted to press the fruit or squeeze the bag, as this will make the jelly cloudy. Leave overnight.

3 Next day, when the dripping has stopped, carefully measure the resulting liquid and return it to the preserving pan along with 450 g (1 lb) caster sugar for each 600 ml (1 pint) of liquid. Stir well over a low heat until the sugar has dissolved completely.

4 Increase the heat and boil rapidly for 10 minutes before testing for a set (page 12). If necessary, boil for a further minute then test again. Continue testing at 1-minute intervals, as necessary, until the jelly has reached setting point.

5 Remove the pan from the heat, skim off any scum and allow the jelly to cool briefly. Carefully pour into hot sterilised jars (page 9). Seal the jars and allow the jelly to cool completely before labelling and storing.

Cranberry and Port Jelly

Makes: *5 x 225 ml (8 fl oz) jars*
Preparation & cooking time: *1 hour + straining overnight*

A gorgeous jelly, this is fruity and spicy, with a flavour of port. It is fabulous in a cold chicken sandwich.

1.5 kg (3 lb 5 oz) cranberries
1 cinnamon stick
a few juniper berries
2 cloves
strip of orange zest
preserving sugar (see step 3 for quantity)
500 ml (18 fl oz) ruby port

1 Put the cranberries, cinnamon stick, juniper berries, cloves, orange zest and port into a large pan or preserving pan. Add enough water to barely cover and bring to the boil. Simmer over a gentle heat for 25–30 minutes, or until the cranberries have burst and become tender. Mash well, using a potato masher, to extract as much juice as possible.

2 Strain through a jelly bag or muslin-lined nylon sieve set over a large bowl. Do not be tempted to press the fruit or squeeze the bag, as this will cause the jelly to become cloudy. Leave overnight.

3 Next day, when the dripping has stopped, carefully measure the resulting liquid and return it to the pan along with 275 g (10 oz) preserving sugar for each 600 ml (1 pint) of liquid. Stir well over a low heat until the sugar has dissolved completely. Add the port.

4 Increase the heat and boil rapidly for 10–15 minutes before testing for a set (page 12). If necessary, boil for a further minute then test again. Continue testing at 1-minute intervals, as necessary, until the jelly has reached setting point.

5 Remove the pan from the heat, skim off any scum and allow the jelly to cool briefly. Carefully pour the jelly into hot sterilised jars (page 9). Seal the jars and allow the jelly to cool completely before labelling and storing.

Mint Jelly

Makes: *9 x 225 ml (8 fl oz) jars*
Preparation & cooking time: *1 hour + straining overnight*

The classic jelly to accompany roast lamb, it's a beautiful colour too.

1.5 kg (3 lb 5 oz) cooking apples
juice of 3 lemons
50 g (2 oz) fresh mint
a few drops of green food colouring (optional)
caster sugar (see step 3 for quantity)

1 Wash and roughly chop the apples without peeling them. Finely chop half of the mint. Place the apples into a heavy bottomed saucepan with just enough water to cover. Add the juice of the lemons and the chopped mint, bring to the boil and simmer for around 20–30 minutes, or until the apples are soft.

2 Spoon the apple pulp into a muslin-lined nylon sieve or jelly bag suspended over a large bowl. Don't be tempted to press the fruit or squeeze the bag, as this will make the jelly cloudy. Leave overnight.

3 Next day, when the dripping has stopped, carefully measure the resulting liquid and return it to the preserving pan along with 450 g (1 lb) caster sugar for each 600 ml (1 pint) of liquid. Stir well over a low heat until the sugar has dissolved completely.

4 Increase the heat and boil rapidly for 10–15 minutes before testing for a set (page 12). If necessary, boil for a further minute then test again. Continue testing at 1-minute intervals, as necessary, until the jelly has reached setting point.

5 Remove from the heat, skim off any scum and allow the jelly to cool briefly before adding the remaining mint, finely chopped, and 2 or 3 drops of green food colouring, if using. Carefully pour the jelly into hot sterilised jars (page 9). Seal the jars and allow the jelly to cool completely before labelling and storing.

Rosehip Jelly

Makes: *about 3 x 225 ml (8 fl oz) jars*
Preparation and cooking time: *45 minutes + straining overnight*

Rosehips have a surprising flavour, quite sharp and lemony but with a lovely fragrance too. I managed to find a wild rose, which always has little bright orange hips in the autumn, growing in a neighbour's front garden. I asked permission, of course … A rosehip is ripe if it is brightly coloured and soft but not squishy.

500 g (1 lb 2 oz) ripe rose hips (from *rugosa* **roses, if possible), stray leaves, stems and flowers removed**
2 tablespoons lemon juice
1 kg (2 lb 4 oz) crab or cooking apples, roughly chopped, including cores, pips and skin
caster sugar (see step 3 for quantity)

1 Wash and drain the rose hips. Chop roughly and put into a large pan or preserving pan with the lemon juice, apples (including cores, pips and skin) and enough water to just cover. Bring to a boil and simmer for about 30 minutes until soft. Mash thoroughly to extract as much juice as possible.

2 Strain through a jelly bag or muslin-lined nylon sieve, set over a large bowl. Do not be tempted to press the fruit or squeeze the bag as this will cause the jelly to become cloudy. Leave until the dripping has stopped. This may take several hours or even overnight.

3 Next day, when the dripping has stopped, carefully measure the resulting liquid and return it to the pan along with 450 g (1 lb) caster sugar for each 600 ml (1 pint) of liquid. Stir well over a low heat until the sugar has dissolved completely.

4 Increase the heat and boil rapidly for 5–10 minutes before testing for a set (page 12). If necessary, boil for a further minute then test again. Continue testing at 1-minute intervals, as necessary, until the jelly has reached setting point.

5 Remove from the heat, skim off any scum, and allow the jelly to cool briefly. Carefully pour the jelly into hot sterilised jars (page 9). Seal the jars and allow the jelly to cool completely before labelling and storing.

Apple and Rosemary Jelly

Makes: *9 x 225 ml (8 fl oz) jars*
Preparation & cooking time: *1 hour + straining overnight*

Although this is quite a sweet, fruity jelly, the addition of the rosemary really lifts it. Try it with roast pork.

1.5 kg (3 lb 5 oz) cooking apples
juice of 3 lemons
4 bushy sprigs rosemary, bruised
granulated sugar (see step 3 for quantity)

1   Wash the apples and, without peeling them, chop roughly. Place the apples into a heavy-bottomed saucepan with just enough water to cover. Add the juice of the lemons and the rosemary, bring to the boil and simmer for around 20–30 minutes, or until the apples are soft.

2   Spoon the apple pulp into a muslin-lined nylon sieve or jelly bag suspended over a large bowl. Don't be tempted to press the fruit or squeeze the bag, as this will make the jelly cloudy. Leave overnight.

3   Next day, when the dripping has stopped, carefully measure the resulting liquid and return it to the preserving pan along with 450 g (1 lb) granulated sugar for each 600 ml (1 pint) of liquid. Stir well over a low heat until the sugar has dissolved completely.

4   Increase the heat and boil rapidly for 10–15 minutes before testing for a set (page 12). If necessary, boil for another minute then test again. Continue testing at 1-minute intervals, as necessary, until the jelly has reached setting point.

5   Remove from the heat, skim off any scum and allow the jelly to cool briefly. Carefully pour into hot sterilised jars (page 9). Seal the jars and allow the jelly to cool completely before labelling and storing.

Tomato Jelly

Makes: *9 x 225 ml (8 fl oz) jars*
Preparation & cooking time: *50 minutes + straining overnight*

This is another unusual jelly, which is very good served with cold roast meat as an alternative to redcurrant or mint jelly.

1.5 kg (3 lb 5 oz) ripe tomatoes
2 Granny Smith apples, unpeeled and roughly
    chopped (keep the pips and core)
25 g (1 oz) fresh basil
3 tablespoons lemon juice
granulated sugar (see step 3 for quantity)

1 Wipe the tomatoes and chop roughly. Put into a large pan or preserving pan along with the apples, half the basil and just enough water to barely cover. Bring to a boil and simmer gently for about 20 minutes until the tomatoes and apples are soft and pulpy. Mash with a potato masher to extract as much juice as possible.

2 Spoon the pulp into a muslin-lined nylon sieve or jelly bag suspended over a large bowl. Don't be tempted to press or squeeze the bag, as this will make the jelly cloudy. Leave overnight.

3 Next day, when the dripping has stopped, carefully measure the resulting liquid and return it to the preserving pan along with the lemon juice and 450 g (1 lb) caster sugar for each 600 ml (1 pint) of liquid. Stir well over a low heat until the sugar has dissolved completely.

4 Increase the heat and boil rapidly for 10–15 minutes before testing for a set (page 12). If necessary, boil for another minute then test again. Continue testing at 1-minute intervals, as necessary, until the jelly has reached setting point.

5 Remove from the heat, skim off any scum and allow the jelly to cool briefly. Add the remaining basil, finely shredded. Carefully pour the jelly into hot sterilised jars (page 9). Seal the jars and allow the jelly to cool completely before labelling and storing.

Marmalades and Mincemeat

By EU definition, marmalade must be made with citrus fruit, thanks largely to the British obsession with it (other European languages use a word with a similar root to marmalade to refer to all gelled fruit spreads, not just citrus-based ones). The most popular marmalade is made with Seville oranges, which are small, bitter oranges grown in the south of Spain. The Seville orange has a thick, rough skin and very tart flesh, full of seeds. They also contain lots of pectin, making them a good choice for a well-set marmalade. Unfortunately, Seville oranges have a very short season; they're only available for a few short weeks in January. Fortunately, there are lots of other citrus fruits available, almost all of which can be successfully made into marmalades. You'll find Seville Orange Marmalade in this chapter, but also Lemon and Pink Grapefruit, Mandarin, Pineapple and Rum, and even Strawberry Lemon-Lime marmalades – as well as classic Christmas Mincemeat.

Seville Orange Marmalade

Makes: *9 x 225 ml (8 fl oz) jars*
Preparation & cooking time: *2¾ hours*

1 kg (2 lb 4 oz) Seville oranges
1 lemon
2 kg (4 lb 8 oz) granulated sugar

1 Measure 2.25 litres (4 pints) water into a large pan or preserving pan.

2 To prepare the oranges and lemon, cut them into quarters. Squeeze the juice into the pan along with the water. Reserve the membranes and any pips and set aside on a large square of muslin.

3 Cut the peel from the oranges and lemon into thin shreds, adding them to the pan as you go. Tie up the reserved pips and membranes in the muslin and tie this bag to the handle of the pan (this will make it easier to remove later) so that it is suspended in the water.

4 Bring the liquid up to boiling point and simmer gently, uncovered, for 2 hours, or until the peel is completely soft (it should squash easily between your fingers).

5 Remove the bag of pips and set aside. Add the sugar to the pan and stir over a low heat until completely dissolved – if you're not sure, carry on stirring for a few minutes longer. Any crystals of sugar will cause the marmalade to crystallize so try not to rush this step.

6 Now increase the heat and squeeze the bag of pips on the side of the pan to extract all the pectin – you'll see it ooze out. Whisk this into the mixture.

7 As soon as the mixture reaches a fast boil, start a timer. After 15 minutes, test for a set (page 12). If necessary, continue testing at 5-minute intervals until the marmalade has reached setting point.

8 Remove from the heat, skim off any scum, and allow the marmalade to cool briefly. Carefully pour it into hot sterilised jars (page 9). Seal the jars and allow to cool completely before labelling and storing.

Microwave Sweet Orange Marmalade

Cut 275 g (9½ oz) oranges and 1 lemon into quarters. Squeeze the juice from the oranges and lemon into a large microwaveable bowl. Remove and reserve the pips as above, adding the squeezed-out lemon shells too. Finely slice the orange peel and put it into the bowl, along with the bag of pips and 300 ml (½ pint) boiling water. Leave to stand for 1 hour. Add a further 200 ml (7 fl oz) boiling water and microwave on high for 20 minutes, stirring halfway, until the peel is tender. Add 500 g (1 lb 2 oz) preserving or jam sugar and stir until dissolved. Microwave on high for a further 25 minutes, stirring every 5 minutes, until the setting point is reached (page 12). Pour the marmalade into jars as above.

Lemon and Pink Grapefruit Marmalade

Makes: *9 x 225 ml (8 fl oz) jars*
Preparation & cooking time: *2¾ hours*

I first made this many years ago for a photo shoot I was working on and found it utterly delicious – I think the succulence of the grapefruit peel is what makes it so successful.

3 large pink or red grapefruit
2 large lemons
2 kg (4lb 8 oz) granulated sugar

1 Measure 2.25 litres (4 pints) water into a large pan or preserving pan.

2 To prepare the grapefruit and lemons, cut the fruit into quarters. Squeeze the juice into the pan along with the water. Reserve the membranes and any pips and set aside on a large square of muslin.

3 Cut the peel from the grapefruit and lemons into thin shreds, adding them to the pan as you go. Tie up the reserved pips and membranes in the muslin and tie this bag in turn to the handle of the pan (this will make it easier to remove later) so that the bag is suspended in the water.

4 Bring the liquid up to boiling point and simmer gently, uncovered, for 2 hours, or until the peel is completely soft (it should squash easily between your fingers).

5 Remove the bag of pips and set aside. Add the sugar to the pan and stir over a low heat until completely dissolved – if you're not sure, carry on stirring for a few minutes longer. Any crystals of sugar will cause the marmalade to crystallize so try not to rush this step.

6 Now increase the heat and squeeze the bag of pips on the side of the pan to extract all the pectin – you'll see it ooze out. Whisk this into the mixture.

7 As soon as the mixture reaches a fast boil, start a timer. After 15 minutes, test for a set (page 12). If necessary, continue testing at 5-minute intervals until the marmalade has reached setting point.

8 Remove the pan from the heat, skim off any scum and allow it to cool briefly. Carefully pour the marmalade into hot sterilised jars (page 9). Seal the jars and allow the marmalade to cool completely before labelling and storing.

Ugli Fruit Marmalade

Makes: *9 x 225 ml (8 fl oz) jars*
Preparation & cooking time: *2¾ hours*

Ugli fruit are thought to be a natural hybrid of the grapefruit and mandarin, and are grown in Jamaica. Because ugli fruit are sweeter than grapefruit, the addition of lemon is essential to give this marmalade its sharp edge.

1 kg (2 lb 4 oz) ugli fruit
2 large lemons
2 kg (4 lb 8 oz) granulated sugar

1 Measure 2.25 litres (4 pints) water into a large pan or preserving pan.

2 To prepare the ugli fruit and lemons, cut them into quarters. Squeeze the juice into the pan along with the water. Reserve the membranes and any pips and set aside on a large square of muslin.

3 Cut the peel from the ugli fruit and lemons into thin shreds, adding them to the pan as you go. Tie up the reserved pips and membranes in the muslin and tie this bag in turn to the handle of the pan (this will make it easier to remove later) so that the bag is suspended in the water.

4 Bring the liquid up to boiling point and simmer gently, uncovered, for 2 hours or until the peel is completely soft (it should squash easily between your fingers).

5 Remove the bag of pips and set aside. Add the sugar to the pan and stir over a low heat until completely dissolved – if you're not sure, carry on stirring a few minutes longer. Any crystals of sugar will cause the marmalade to crystallize so don't try to rush this step.

6 Increase the heat and squeeze the bag of pips on the side of the pan to extract all the pectin. Whisk this into the mixture.

7 As soon as the mixture reaches a fast boil, start a timer. After 15 minutes, test for a set (page 12). If necessary, continue testing at 5-minute intervals until the marmalade has reached setting point.

8 Remove from the heat, skim off any scum, and allow the marmalade to cool briefly. Carefully pour the marmalade into hot sterilised jars (page 9). Seal the jars and allow the marmalade to cool completely before labelling and storing.

Kumquat Marmalade

Makes: *9 x 225 ml (8 fl oz) jars*
Preparation & cooking time: *2¾ hours*

This is a very pretty marmalade, with little circles of kumquat. Pot into pretty jars and give as an unusual gift.

750 g (1 lb 10 oz) kumquats
2 oranges
2 kg (4 lb 8 oz) granulated sugar
1 tablespoon coriander seeds, lightly crushed

1 Measure 2.25 litres (4 pints) water into a large pan or preserving pan.

2 To prepare the kumquats, slice them thinly crosswise, removing and reserving any pips on a large square of muslin. Add the flesh to the pan. Cut the oranges lengthways into quarters. Squeeze the juice into the pan along with the water. Reserve the membranes and any pips and squeezed-out shells and set aside along the kumquat pips.

3 Tie the reserved pips and membranes up in the muslin and tie this bag to the handle of the pan (this will make it easier to remove later) so that the bag is suspended in the water.

4 Bring the mixture to boiling point and simmer gently, uncovered, for 2 hours, or until the peel is completely soft (it should squash easily between your fingers).

5 Remove the bag of pips and set aside. Add the sugar and coriander seeds to the pan and stir over a low heat until the sugar is completely dissolved – if you're not sure, carry on stirring for a few minutes longer. Any crystals of sugar will cause the marmalade to crystallize so try not to rush this step.

6 Now increase the heat and squeeze the bag of pips on the side of the pan to extract all the pectin – you'll see it ooze out. Whisk this into the mixture.

7 As soon as the mixture reaches a fast boil, start a timer. After 15 minutes, test for a set (page 12). If necessary, continue testing at 5-minute intervals until the marmalade has reached setting point.

8 Remove from the heat, skim off any scum, and allow the mixture to cool briefly. Carefully pour into hot sterilised jars (page 9. Seal the jars and allow the marmalade to cool completely before labelling and storing.

Zesty Blueberry Marmalade

Makes: *5 x 225 ml (8 fl oz) jars*
Preparation & cooking time: *2¾ hours*

The unusual addition of blueberries turns this marmalade
a jewel-bright shade of purple.

1 orange
1 lemon
1 lime
**450 g (1 lb) fresh blueberries (you can use
frozen, thawed blueberries also)**
1 kg (2 lb 4 oz) granulated sugar

1 Measure 1.5 litres (2½ pints) water into a large
pan or preserving pan.

2 To prepare the orange, lemon and lime, cut
them lengthways into quarters. Squeeze
the juice into the pan along with the water.
Reserve the membranes and any pips and set
aside on a large square of muslin.

3 Cut the peel from the orange, lemon and lime
into thin shreds, adding them to the pan as
you go. Tie the reserved pips and membranes
up in the muslin and tie this bag in turn to the
handle of the pan (this will make it easier to
remove later) so that the bag is suspended in
the water.

4 Bring the liquid up to boiling point and simmer
gently, uncovered, for 2 hours, or until the
peel is completely soft (it should squash easily
between your fingers).

5 Remove the bag of pips and set aside. Add
the blueberries and sugar to the pan and stir
over a low heat until the sugar is completely
dissolved – if you're not sure, carry on stirring
for a few minutes longer. Any crystals of sugar
will cause the marmalade to crystallize so try
not to rush this step.

6 Now increase the heat and squeeze the bag
of pips on the side of the pan to extract all the
pectin – you'll see it ooze out. Whisk this into
the mixture.

7 As soon as the mixture reaches a fast boil,
start a timer. After 15 minutes, test for a set
(page 12). If necessary, continue testing at
5-minute intervals until the marmalade has
reached setting point.

8 Remove the pan from the heat, skim off any
scum and allow the marmalade to cool briefly.
Carefully pour the mixture into hot sterilised
jars (page 9). Seal the jars and allow the
marmalade to cool completely before labelling
and storing.

Mandarin, Pineapple and Rum Marmalade

Makes: *9 x 225 ml (8 fl oz) jars*
Preparation & cooking time: *2¾ hours*

Use only tinned pineapple for this recipe as fresh pineapple contains an enzyme that prevents the marmalade from setting.

750 g (1lb 10 oz) mandarins
2 lemons
500 g (1 lb 2 oz) tinned pineapple chunks in juice (drained weight)
2 kg (4 lb 8 oz) light muscovado sugar
100 ml (3½ fl oz) dark rum

1 Measure 2.25 litres (4 pints) water into a large pan or preserving pan.

2 To prepare the mandarins and lemons, cut them into quarters. Squeeze the juice into the pan along with the water. Reserve the mandarin membranes and any pips and set aside on a large square of muslin along with the squeezed–out lemon shells.

3 Cut the peel from the mandarins into thin shreds, adding them to the pan as you go. Tie up the reserved pips, membranes and lemon shells in the muslin and tie this bag in turn to the handle of the pan (this will make it easier to remove later) so that the bag is suspended in the water.

4 Bring the liquid up to boiling point and simmer gently, uncovered, for 2 hours, or until the peel is completely soft (it should squash easily between your fingers).

5 Remove the bag of pips and set aside. Add the pineapple and sugar to the pan and stir over a low heat until the sugar is completely dissolved – if you're not sure, carry on stirring for a few minutes longer. Any crystals of sugar will cause the marmalade to crystallize so try not to rush this step.

6 Now increase the heat and squeeze the bag of pips on the side of the pan to extract all the pectin – you'll see it ooze out. Whisk this into the mixture.

7 As soon as the mixture reaches a fast boil, start a timer. After 15 minutes, test for a set (page 12). If necessary, continue testing at 5-minute intervals until the marmalade has reached setting point.

8 Remove from the heat, skim off any scum, and allow the mixture to cool briefly. Add the rum. Carefully pour the marmalade into hot sterilised jars (page 9). Seal the jars and allow the marmalade to cool completely before labelling and storing.

Blood Orange Marmalade

Makes: *9 x 225 ml (8 fl oz) jars*
Preparation & cooking time: *2¾ hours*

This marmalade is equally successful with blush oranges, which tend to be sweeter with a lovely pinkish tinge to the flesh.

1 kg (2 lb 4 oz) blood oranges
1 lemon
2 kg (4 lb 8 oz) granulated sugar
½ x 250 ml (9 fl oz) bottle liquid pectin

1 Measure 2.25 litres (4 pints) water into a large pan or preserving pan.

2 To prepare the oranges and lemon, cut them into quarters. Squeeze the juice into the pan along with the water. Reserve the membranes and any pips and set aside on a large square of muslin.

3 Cut the peel from both the oranges and lemon into thin shreds, adding them to the pan as you go. Tie up the reserved pips and membranes in the muslin and tie this bag in turn to the handle of the pan (this will make it easier to remove later) so that the bag is suspended in the water.

4 Bring the liquid to boiling point and simmer gently, uncovered, for 2 hours, or until the peel is completely soft (it should squash easily between your fingers).

5 Remove the bag of pips and set aside. Add the sugar to the pan and stir over a low heat until completely dissolved – if you're not sure, carry on stirring for a few minutes longer. Any crystals of sugar will cause the marmalade to crystallize so don't try to rush this step.

6 Now increase the heat and squeeze the bag of pips on the side of the pan to extract all the pectin – you'll see it ooze out. Add the liquid pectin and whisk this into the mixture for 1 minute.

7 As soon as the mixture reaches a fast boil, start a timer. After 15 minutes, test for a set. (page 12). If necessary, continue testing at 5-minute intervals until the marmalade has reached setting point.

8 Remove the pan from the heat, skim off any scum, and allow the mixture to cool briefly. Carefully pour into hot sterilised jars (page 9). Seal the jars and allow the marmalade to cool completely before labelling and storing.

Strawberry Lemon-lime Marmalade

Makes: *4 x 225 ml (8 fl oz) jars*
Preparation & cooking time: *2 hours*

Another unusual marmalade, this time with the addition of fresh strawberries, which cut through the bitterness from the lemons and limes.

2 lemons
4 limes
500 g (1 lb 2 oz) strawberries, wiped, hulled
  and roughly chopped
1 kg (2 lb 4 oz) granulated sugar

1 Measure 1 litre (1¾ pints) of water into a large pan or preserving pan.

2 To prepare the lemons and limes, cut them into quarters. Squeeze the juice into the pan along with the water. Reserve the membranes and any pips and set aside on a large square of muslin.

3 Cut the peel from the lemons and limes into thin shreds, adding them to the pan as you go. Tie the reserved pips and membranes up in the muslin bag and tie this in turn to the handle of the pan (this will make it easier to remove later) so that the bag is suspended in the water.

4 Bring the liquid to boiling point and simmer gently, uncovered, for 1 – 1½ hours or until the peel is completely soft (it should squash easily between your fingers).

5 Remove the bag of pips and set aside. Add the strawberries and sugar to the pan and stir over a low heat until the sugar is completely dissolved – if you're not sure, carry on stirring for a few minutes longer. Any crystals of sugar will cause the marmalade to crystallize so try not to rush this step.

6 Now increase the heat and squeeze the bag of pips on the side of the pan to extract all the pectin – you'll see it ooze out. Whisk this into the mixture.

7 As soon as the mixture reaches a fast boil, start a timer. After 15 minutes, test for a set (page 12). If necessary, continue testing at 5-minute intervals until the marmalade has reached setting point.

8 Remove the pan from the heat, skim off any scum, and allow the mixture to cool briefly. Carefully pour into hot sterilised jars (page 9). Seal the jars and allow the marmalade to cool completely before labelling and storing.

Christmas Mincemeat with Brandy

Makes: *1 x 1.5 litre jar*
Preparation and cooking time: *3 hours 20 minutes + macerating overnight and cooling*

Mincemeat is something of a moveable feast. Adjust the quantities of dried fruit according to your preference – more or less raisins or currants won't make a difference. The classic problem with mincemeat is that because of the fresh apple, which starts to ferment after a couple of months (or sooner), it has a relatively short shelf life. You can get around this by gently heating the whole lot until the suet melts and coats everything. This coating seems to stop the apples fermenting, although I have always stored my mincemeat in the refrigerator in any case.

500 g (1 lb 2 oz) raisins
250 g (9 oz) sultanas
250 g (9 oz) currants
125 g (4 oz) candied peel (page 115), chopped
350 g (12 oz) soft brown sugar
juice and finely grated zest of 1 lemon
juice and finely grated zest of 1 orange
2 Bramley apples, cored and diced
250 g (9 oz) suet (use vegetarian if you wish)
50 g (2 oz) blanched almonds, roughly chopped
75 g (2 oz) glacé cherries, roughly chopped
1 teaspoon mixed spice
1 teaspoon ground cinnamon
½ teaspoon freshly grated nutmeg
150 ml (¼ pint) brandy

1 The day before you want to bottle your mincemeat, mix everything together, except the brandy, in a very large non-metallic (ceramic, glass or earthenware) bowl. Cover with a clean tea towel and leave overnight.

2 Next day, preheat the oven to a low heat (Gas Mark ¼/110°C/225°F). Remove the tea towel from the bowl and replace with foil. Put the bowl into the oven and leave for about 3 hours until all the suet has melted. Remove from the oven and allow the mixture to cool completely, stirring occasionally.

3 When completely cold, stir in the brandy and pack into warm sterilised jars and seal. Label the jars before storing. Mincemeat made in this way will keep successfully for years – I have some in the fridge that I made 3 years ago (I hope to finish it this year!)

Exotic Fruit Mincemeat with Rum

Makes: *1 x 1.5 litre jar*
Preparation & cooking time: *3 hours, 20 minutes + macerating overnight and cooling*

Fancy a change from the standard mincemeat? This version uses exotic dried fruits, which have become increasingly available in recent years, to produce an interesting variation on a theme.

1 kg (2 lb 4 oz) mixed dried exotic fruits, including pineapple, mango, figs, peaches, apricots and papaya, chopped into small dice
50 g (2 oz) desiccated coconut
350 g (12 oz) dark muscovado sugar
juice and finely grated zest of 1 lemon
juice and finely grated zest of 1 orange
1 Bramley apple, cored and coarsely grated
250 g (9 oz) suet (use vegetarian if you wish)
50 g (2 oz) blanched almonds, roughly chopped
1 teaspoon allspice
1 teaspoon ground cinnamon
150 ml (¼ pint) dark rum

1 Mix everything together, except the rum, in a large, non-metallic bowl. Cover with a clean tea towel and leave to stand overnight.

2 Next day, preheat the oven to a low heat (Gas Mark ¼/110°C/225°F). Remove the tea towel from the bowl and replace with foil. Put the bowl into the oven and leave for about 3 hours until all the suet has melted. Remove from the oven and allow the mixture to cool completely, stirring occasionally.

3 When completely cold, stir in the rum. Pack the mincemeat into cold sterilised jars and seal. Label the jars before storing.

Curds and Cheeses

Curds are, perhaps, a special case. Not really preserves (you can't keep them for longer than a few weeks) we nonetheless use them in the same way – spread on toast and as fillings for cakes and other desserts. They are simple to make, requiring only that you stir gently for 20 minutes or so, after which time they miraculously turn thick and gelatinous, perfect for spreading. In this chapter you'll find a recipe for lemon curd, but also curds made with lime, orange, passion fruit, mango, raspberries, gooseberries and pineapple. Any fruit with a slight sharpness makes a good curd. There are other useful recipes here too, such as Membrillo (or quince cheese), made by slowly cooking fragrant quinces until they are thick enough to set, and Apple Butter – a delicious treat on toast or American-style pancakes.

Lemon Curd

Makes: *4 x 225 ml (8 fl oz) jars*
Preparation & cooking time: *30 minutes*

325 g (11½ oz) golden caster sugar
juice and finely grated zest of 4 lemons
125 g (4 oz) unsalted butter, cut into
   small pieces
4 eggs, lightly beaten

1 Put the sugar, juice and zest, butter and eggs
   into a large heatproof bowl on top of a pan
   of simmering water. The bottom of the bowl
   mustn't touch the water. Stir constantly with
   a wooden spoon until the mixture is thick and
   coats the back of the spoon.

2 Pour the curd into hot sterilised jars (page 9),
   cover and seal. Label the jars when cold and
   refrigerate for up to 2 weeks. Once opened,
   use within 3 days.

To make the beautiful dessert we have pictured
(right), bake a sheet of ready-rolled puff pastry
between two baking sheets at Gas Mark 6/
200°C/400°F for about 15 minutes until golden
brown. Allow to cool, then cut into three equal
rectangles (use a ruler if necessary). Set aside
the best looking piece, then spread one of the
others with a good layer of lemon curd and top
with some softly whipped cream. Repeat with
another piece of pastry, more lemon curd and
cream. Put on top of the first piece then top the
whole thing with the good-looking pastry and
dust with icing sugar. Use a serrated knife to cut
into slices – and *voila*!

Lime Curd

Makes: *3 x 225 ml (8 fl oz) jars*
Preparation & cooking time: *30 minutes*

Just like lemon, only with
limes… this would also go
well in the dessert described
in the Lemon Curd recipe.

225 g (8 oz) caster sugar
juice and finely grated zest of 5 limes
150 g (5 oz) unsalted butter, cut into
   small pieces
2 large eggs and 2 egg yolks, lightly
   beaten together

1 Put the sugar, juice and zest, butter and eggs
   into a large heatproof bowl on top of a pan
   of simmering water. The bottom of the bowl
   must not touch the water. Stir constantly with
   a wooden spoon until the mixture is thick and
   coats the back of the spoon.

2 Pour the curd into hot sterilised jars (page 9),
   cover and seal. Label the jars when cold and
   refrigerate for up to 2 weeks. Once opened,
   use within 3 days.

Passion Fruit Curd

Makes: *4 x 225 ml (8 fl oz) jars*
Preparation & cooking time: *30 minutes*

This is an absolute stunner. Use this to fill meringue nests then top with a dollop of whipped cream for a quick dessert.

6 passion fruit
125 g (4½ oz) golden caster sugar
50 g (2 oz) unsalted butter, cut into small pieces
3 eggs, plus 3 extra yolks, lightly beaten together

1 Halve the passion fruit and scoop out the pulp into a food processor. Pulse briefly (this helps to loosen the pulp from the seeds) then transfer to a sieve set over a small bowl. Rub the pulp through to remove the seeds.

2 Put the passion fruit pulp, sugar, butter and eggs into a large heatproof bowl on top of a pan of simmering water. The bottom of the bowl mustn't touch the water. Stir constantly with a wooden spoon until the mixture is thick and coats the back of the spoon.

3 Pour the curd into hot sterilised jars (page 9), cover and seal. Label the jars when cold and refrigerate for up to 2 weeks. Once opened, use within 3 days.

Orange Curd

Makes: *4 x 225 ml (8 fl oz) jars*
Preparation & cooking time: *30 minutes*

Sweeter than lemon curd, this makes a nice change. Use sharper varieties of orange, like blood oranges, for this recipe if possible.

150 g (5½ oz) caster sugar
juice and finely grated zest of 2 medium oranges
juice of 1 lemon
100 g (3½ oz) unsalted butter, cut into small pieces
4 large eggs, lightly beaten

1 Put the sugar, orange zest and orange and lemon juices, butter and eggs into a large heatproof bowl on top of a pan of simmering water. The bottom of the bowl mustn't touch the water. Stir constantly with a wooden spoon until the mixture is thick and coats the back of the spoon.

2 Pour the curd into hot sterilised jars (page 9), cover and seal. Label when cold and refrigerate for up to 2 weeks. Once opened, use within 3 days.

Mango Curd

Makes: *4 x 225 ml (8 fl oz) jars*
Preparation & cooking time: *30 minutes*

The velvety nature of puréed mango gives this curd a wonderful texture and unusual flavour.

1 ripe mango (about 450 g/1 lb)
juice and finely grated zest of 1 lime
125 g (4½ oz) golden caster sugar
125 g (4½ oz) unsalted butter, cut into
    small pieces
4 egg yolks, lightly beaten

1 To prepare the mango, remove the peel using a potato peeler then remove the two 'cheeks' of flesh from either side of the central flat stone. Remove any remaining flesh clinging to the stone and put all of it into a food processor or blender. Process the mango flesh until smooth.

2 Put the puréed mango flesh, lime zest and juice, sugar, butter and egg yolks into a large heatproof bowl on top of a pan of simmering water. The bottom of the bowl mustn't touch the water. Stir constantly with a wooden spoon until the mixture is thick and coats the back of the spoon.

3 Pour the curd into hot sterilised jars (page 9), cover and seal. Label the jars when cold and refrigerate for up to 2 weeks. Once opened, use within 3 days.

Gooseberry Curd

Makes: *4 x 225 ml (8 fl oz) jars*
Preparation & cooking time: *30 minutes*

Gooseberries have to be the unsung heroes of the summer. Tangy, sharp, fruity, fragrant – just what you need in a curd.

500 g (1 lb 2 oz) green gooseberries
125 g (4 oz) unsalted butter, cut into
    small pieces
350 g (12 oz) sugar
3 large eggs, lightly beaten

1 Top and tail the gooseberries. Put them into a heavy bottomed saucepan with enough water to just cover. Bring to the boil and simmer until tender. Use a blender or liquidiser to produce a purée. Push the gooseberries through a sieve, making sure you scrape the purée from the underside of the sieve.

2 Put the puréed gooseberries, butter, sugar and eggs into a large heatproof bowl on top of a pan of simmering water. The bottom of the bowl mustn't touch the water. Stir constantly with a wooden spoon until the mixture is thick and coats the back of the spoon.

3 Pour the curd into hot sterilised jars (page 9), cover and seal. Label the jars when cold and refrigerate for up to 2 weeks. Once opened, use within 3 days

Blackberry or Raspberry Curd

Makes: *4 x 225 ml (8 fl oz) jars*
Preparation & cooking time: *30 minutes*

500 g (1 lb 2 oz) blackberries or raspberries
4 tablespoons water
125 g (4½ oz) golden caster sugar
2 tablespoons cornflour
4 egg yolks plus 2 whole eggs, lightly beaten
125 g (4½ oz) unsalted butter, cut into
    small pieces
1 tablespoon lemon juice

1 Put the blackberries or raspberries into a large pan with the water. Bring to the boil, cover and simmer gently for about 20 minutes until the fruit is quite soft. Transfer to a food processor or blender and purée.

2 Press the resulting purée through a nylon sieve into a large heatproof bowl. Allow it to cool for about 10 minutes, so that the eggs don't cook as soon as they hit the purée.

3 Add the sugar, cornflour, eggs, butter and lemon juice. Put the bowl over a pan of simmering water. The bottom of the bowl mustn't touch the water. Stir constantly with a wooden spoon until the mixture is thick and coats the back of the spoon.

4 Pour the curd into hot sterilised jars (page 9), cover and seal. Label the jars when cold and refrigerate for up to 2 weeks. Once opened, use within 3 days.

Pineapple Curd

Makes: *4 x 225 ml (8 fl oz) jars*
Preparation & cooking time: *30 minutes*

This recipe uses pineapple juice, rather than puréed fruit, giving it a texture similar to lemon curd.

100 g (3½ oz) golden caster sugar
2 tablespoons cornflour
300 ml (½ pint) pineapple juice
2 tablespoons lemon juice
100 g (3½ oz) unsalted butter, cut into
    small pieces
3 large eggs, lightly beaten

1 Put the sugar, cornflour, both juices, butter and eggs into a large heatproof bowl on top of a pan of simmering water. The bottom of the bowl mustn't touch the water. Stir constantly with a wooden spoon until thick and the mixture coats the back of the spoon.

2 Pour the curd into hot sterilised jars (page 9), cover and seal. Label the jars when cold and refrigerate for up to 2 weeks. Once opened, use within 3 days.

Apple Butter

Makes: *2 x 225 ml (8 fl oz) jars*
Preparation & cooking time: *1¼ hours*

This is not actually butter, but a soft, slow-cooked spiced apple spread, delicious on hot buttered toast. It's very popular in North America, where there are small towns that organize whole festivals around it.

1.25 kg (3 lb) apples, such as Bramleys
300 ml (½ pint) apple juice or water
100 g (3½ oz) light brown soft sugar
175–200 g (6–7 oz) granulated sugar
 (see step 3)
1 tablespoon ground cinnamon
½ teaspoon ground cloves
¼ teaspoon ground allspice

1 Peel, quarter and core the apples. Put into a large pan or preserving pan with the juice or water. Cover and bring to a boil over a high heat. Reduce the heat and simmer, stirring occasionally, until the apples are very soft, 30–45 minutes. Preheat the oven to Gas Mark 3/170°C/325°F.

2 Transfer the mixture to a blender or food processor, in batches if necessary, and process or blend until smooth.

3 Pour the purée into a 30 x 43 cm (12 x 17 inch) roasting pan. Stir in the brown sugar and add granulated sugar to taste. Mix in the ground cinnamon, cloves and allspice.

4 Bake, uncovered, stirring occasionally for 30–45 minutes, until the mixture is thick enough to mound when spooned onto a plate.

5 Allow the mixture to cool slightly before carefully spooning it into hot sterilised jars (page 9). Seal the jars and allow the apple butter to cool completely before labelling and storing.

Membrillo

Makes: *1 kg (2 lb 4 oz)*
Preparation & cooking time: *2 hours*

1 kg (2 lb 4 oz) quinces, peeled, cored and
    roughly chopped
½ cinnamon stick
1 teaspoon salt
1 kg (2 lb 4 oz) granulated sugar

1 Place the chopped quince in a large pan or
preserving pan. Add the cinnamon stick and
salt and pour in enough water to just cover
the quince.

2 Bring to the boil, reduce the heat and simmer
for 15–20 minutes, until the quince is tender.
Remove the cinnamon stick and discard.

3 Gradually add the sugar and cook, stirring,
over a low heat until completely dissolved.
Continue stirring until the mixture thickens
and darkens to a deep pinky caramel colour,
about 45 minutes. The fruit will be starting
to break down at this stage. Continue
simmering, stirring often, for a further
45 minutes–1 hour until very thick and dark.
Use a potato masher if necessary to make a
smooth purée. For the last 15 minutes or so,
stir constantly so the mixture doesn't catch on
the bottom of the pan.

4 Pour into a lightly greased 900 g (2 lb) loaf tin
and leave to set before cutting into slices.

Pistachio and Fig Cheese

Makes: *1 kg (2 lb 4 oz)*
Preparation & cooking time: *2 hours*

250 g (9 oz) dried figs
250 g (9 oz) caster sugar
1 teaspoon ground cinnamon
½ teaspoon aniseed (from Middle Eastern
    shops), crushed roughly in pestle
    and mortar
2 strips lemon zest
250 g (9 oz) shelled unsalted pistachio nuts

1 Place the dried figs in a large pan or
preserving pan. Barely cover with water and
bring to the boil. Simmer for about 45 minutes
until the fruit is tender.

2 Add the sugar, ground cinnamon, crushed
aniseed and lemon zest. Mix together well
and return to the boil once the sugar has
dissolved. Simmer for a further 45 minutes,
until the mixture is very thick.

3 Meanwhile, toast the pistachios then grind
finely. If necessary, use a hand-held blender to
finely chop the fig mixture in the pan. Add the
ground nuts and stir together well.

4 Return to the boil and simmer, stirring often,
for a further 10 minutes or so until the
mixture is very thick and all the moisture has
evaporated. Pour into a greased 900 g (2 lb)
loaf tin or into individual moulds, as you prefer.
Leave to set before serving.

Chutneys and Relishes

Chutneys have a chequered history, originating in different countries with different styles. For our purposes, chutney is a slow-cooked mixture of fruit and vegetables, with sugar and vinegar, usually spiced, sometimes with the addition of dried fruit. There are countries where chutney is prepared and eaten fresh — Indian coriander chutney springs to mind — but the recipes in this chapter are traditional cooked ones. You'll find Mango Chutney here alongside Apple Chutney, plus some more unusual combinations, such as Date and Banana and Pineapple and Chilli chutneys. A relish is similar to chutney, but cooked for a shorter time with less vinegar. For this reason, a relish will also have more distinct individual ingredients. Cucumber Relish, Sweetcorn and Red Pepper Relish and Ratatouille Relish all feature in this chapter.

Mango Chutney

Makes: *3 x 225 ml (8 fl oz) jars*
Preparation & cooking time: *3½ hours + standing overnight*

The classic Indian chutney, this one has lots of spice and a little bit of heat. Get out your poppadoms …

3 large mangoes, slightly under-ripe (total
   weight about 1.8 kg (4 lb)
350 g (12 oz) soft light brown sugar
½ level teaspoon cumin seeds
1 heaped teaspoon coriander seeds
1 teaspoon black onion seeds (also called
   Nigella seeds or kalonji seeds)
1 teaspoon mustard seeds
2 dried Kashmiri chillies
½ teaspoon ground turmeric
50 g (2 oz) fresh ginger, peeled and grated
400 ml (14 fl oz) malt vinegar
4 cloves garlic, peeled and crushed with
   2 teaspoons salt in a pestle and mortar
1 onion, finely chopped

1 To prepare the mango, remove the peel using a potato peeler then remove the two 'cheeks' of flesh from either side of the central flat stone. Remove any remaining flesh clinging to the stone. Chop the flesh into approximately 2.5 cm (1 inch) cubes – don't worry if they're not exactly square.

2 Put the chopped mango flesh into a large bowl and sprinkle over the sugar. Cover with a clean tea towel and leave to stand overnight.

3 Next day, heat a small frying pan without any oil and add the whole spices, including the dried chillies. Stir-fry for a few minutes until the seeds darken, become fragrant and start to pop. Transfer to a pestle and mortar and crush coarsely. Add the turmeric and set aside.

4 Put the mango, crushed spices and all the remaining ingredients into a large pan or preserving pan. Slowly bring to a gentle simmer and cook gently for 3 hours, stirring occasionally, until the mango becomes translucent and most of the liquid has evaporated. Test if the chutney is ready (page 12). Watch it particularly carefully towards the end of this time in order to prevent it catching.

5 Remove from the heat and leave to stand briefly. Carefully pour into hot sterilised jars (page 9) and seal. Allow the chutney to cool completely before labelling and storing in a cool, dark cupboard. Store for at least 2 months before eating.

Apple Chutney

Makes: *2 x 500 ml (18 fl oz) jars*
Preparation & cooking time: *2½ hours*

This is a spicy apple chutney, perfect for serving with cheese and cold meat.

250 g (9 oz) onions, chopped
1 kg (2 lb 4 oz) cooking apples, cored and
    chopped
125 g (4½ oz) sultanas, raisins or
    chopped dates
1 tablespoon ground coriander
1 tablespoon paprika
1 tablespoon mixed spice
1 tablespoon salt
350 g (12 oz) granulated sugar
700 ml (1¼ pints) malt vinegar

1 Put all the ingredients into a large pan or preserving pan. Slowly bring to the boil, stirring often, until the sugar has completely dissolved.

2 Simmer for 1½–2 hours, stirring from time to time to stop the chutney sticking to the pan.

3 After the shortest cooking time, start checking if the chutney is ready by dragging a channel through the mixture (with a wooden spoon) so that the bottom of the pan is visible. If the channel fills immediately with liquid, the chutney is not ready. Cook for a further 15 minutes and check again. The chutney is ready when the channel does not fill and the mixture is very thick.

4 Remove the pan from the heat and leave to stand briefly. Carefully pour the chutney into hot sterilised jars (page 9) and seal. Allow the chutney to cool completely before labelling and storing in a cool, dark cupboard. Store for at least 2 months before eating.

Beetroot and Horseradish Chutney

Makes: *1 x 500 ml (18 fl oz) jar*
Preparation & cooking time: *2 hours*

Although this is an unusual combination in a chutney, beetroot and horseradish go very well together. Spoon this on to a roast beef sandwich made with thickly sliced white bread.

750 g (1 lb 10 oz) raw beetroot, trimmed, peeled and finely diced
1 onion, chopped
1 dessert apple, cored and chopped
2 tablespoons freshly grated horseradish
200 g (7 oz) golden granulated sugar
300 ml (½ pint) white wine vinegar
2 teaspoons salt

1 Put all the ingredients into a large pan or preserving pan. Bring slowly to the boil, stirring often, until all the sugar has dissolved.

2 Cook gently for a further 1–1½ hours, stirring from time to time to stop the chutney sticking to the pan.

3 After the shortest cooking time, start checking if the chutney is ready by dragging a channel through the mixture so that the bottom of the pan is visible. If the channel fills immediately with liquid, the chutney is not ready. Cook for a further 15 minutes and check again. The chutney is ready when the channel does not fill and the mixture is very thick.

4 Remove the pan from the heat and leave to stand briefly. Carefully pour into hot sterilised jars (page 9) and seal. Allow the chutney to cool completely before labelling and storing in a cool, dark cupboard. Store for at least 2 months before eating.

Spiced Dried Apricot and Cranberry Chutney

Makes: *2 x 500 ml (18 fl oz) jars*
Preparation & cooking time: *30 minutes*

Cranberries have a lot of pectin in them, which means that they reach setting point very quickly – this thick, zingy chutney cooks very quickly indeed.

350 g (12 oz) fresh or frozen cranberries
125 g (4½ oz) granulated sugar
200 g (7 oz) dried apricots, coarsely chopped
75 g (2½ oz) currants
75 g (2½ oz) sultanas
250 ml (9 fl oz) cider vinegar

1 Put the cranberries (if using frozen, there's no need to defrost), sugar, dried fruit and vinegar into a large pan or preserving pan. Bring slowly to the boil, stirring often, until the sugar has completely dissolved.

2 Cook gently for a further 15 minutes, stirring from time to time to stop the chutney sticking to the pan.

3 Check if the chutney is ready by dragging a channel through the mixture (with a wooden spoon) so that the bottom of the pan is visible. If the channel fills immediately with liquid, the chutney is not yet ready. Cook for a further 10 minutes and check again. The chutney is ready when the channel does not fill and the mixture is very thick.

4 Remove the pan from the heat and leave to stand for 20 minutes. Carefully pour into hot sterilised jars (page 9) and seal. Allow the chutney to cool completely before labelling and storing in a cool, dark cupboard. Store for at least 2 months before eating.

Date and Banana Chutney

Makes: *1 x 500 ml (18 fl oz) jar*
Preparation & cooking time: *2 hours*

Try this delicious chutney for a Ploughman's lunch.

250 g (9 oz) fresh dates, stoned and chopped
   (weighed after stoning)
6 bananas, peeled and sliced – use ripe but
   not soft fruit
500 g (1 lb 2 oz) onions, finely chopped
1 dried Kashmiri chilli, crumbled
350 ml (12 fl oz) white wine vinegar
250 g (9 oz) light brown soft sugar
100 g (3½ oz) chopped crystallized ginger

1 Put all the ingredients into a large pan or
preserving pan. Bring slowly to the boil,
stirring often, until all the sugar has dissolved.

2 Cook gently for a further 1–½ hours, stirring
from time to time to stop the chutney sticking
to the pan.

3 After the shortest cooking time, start checking
if the chutney is ready by dragging a channel
through the mixture (with a wooden spoon)
so that the bottom of the pan is visible. If
the channel fills immediately with liquid, the
chutney is not yct ready. Cook for a further
15 minutes and check again. The chutney is
ready when the channel does not fill and the
mixture is very thick.

4 Remove the pan from the heat and leave to
stand briefly. Carefully pour into hot sterilised
jars (page 9) and seal. Allow the chutney to
cool completely before labelling and storing
in a cool, dark cupboard. Store for at least 2
months before eating.

Pineapple and Chilli Chutney

Makes: *1 x 225 ml (8 fl oz) jar*
Preparation & cooking time: *50–60 minutes*

When testing this recipe, I discovered that I had no curry powder in my storecupboard, so I substituted Ras-el-Hanout, a Moroccan blend of curry spices that includes rose petals. I would suggest seeking this out (I bought mine in a large supermarket), as it adds a wonderful fragrance to the chutney. Ordinary curry powder will also work perfectly well, if that's what you have to hand.

1 large onion, chopped
125 g (4½ oz) light brown soft sugar
100 ml (3½ fl oz) white wine vinegar
350 g (12 oz) fresh pineapple, peeled and finely chopped (weighed after peeling)
1 large red finger chilli, de-seeded and finely chopped (leave the seeds in if you like it hot)
2 teaspoons curry powder (or Ras-el-Hanout, see note above)
½ teaspoon ground ginger
½ teaspoon salt

1 Put the onion, sugar, vinegar, pineapple, chilli, spices and salt into a large pan or preserving pan. Bring slowly to the boil, stirring often, until all the sugar has dissolved.

2 Cook gently for about 20–30 minutes until the pineapple is tender and the mixture has thickened.

3 Check if the chutney is ready by dragging a channel through the mixture (with a wooden spoon) so that the bottom of the pan is visible. If the channel fills immediately with liquid, the chutney is not yet ready. Cook for a further 10 minutes and check again. The chutney is ready when the channel does not fill and the mixture is very thick.

4 Remove the pan from the heat and leave to stand briefly. Carefully pour into a hot sterilised jar (page 9) and seal. Allow the chutney to cool completely before labelling and storing in a cool, dark cupboard. Store for at least 2 months before eating.

Green Tomato and Apple Chutney

Makes: *4 x 500 ml (18 fl oz) jars*
Preparation & cooking time: *3–3½ hours*

I have to give credit where credit is due – this recipe was passed to me by my husband's step-mother, whose father used to make it when she was young. I've tweaked it a little, but it's his recipe at heart. So, thank you Don Brabben. (Oh, and it's a very good way to use up those last few tomatoes that just don't quite ripen).

225 g (8 oz) light soft brown sugar
850 ml (1½ pints) malt vinegar
900 g (2 lb) green tomatoes, roughly chopped
900 g (2 lb) Bramley apples, cored and roughly
    chopped
225 g (8 oz) sultanas
115 g (4 oz) raisins
225 g (8 oz) shallots, roughly chopped
juice of 1 lemon
25 g (1 oz) salt
1 teaspoon ground ginger
1 tablespoon ground mixed spice

1 Put the sugar and vinegar into a large pan or preserving pan over a medium heat. Stir often, until the sugar has completely dissolved. Add the remaining ingredients and return the mixture to the boil.

2 Reduce the heat and simmer gently for 2½–3 hours. Check if the chutney is ready by dragging a channel through the mixture (with a wooden spoon) so that the bottom of the pan is visible. If the channel fills immediately with liquid, the chutney is not yet ready. Cook for a further 10 minutes and check again. The chutney is ready when the channel does not fill and the mixture is very thick.

3 Remove the pan from the heat and leave to stand briefly. Carefully pour into hot sterilised jars (page 9) and seal. Allow the chutney to cool completely before labelling and storing in a cool, dark cupboard. Store for at least 2 months before eating.

Spiced Tomato Chutney

Makes: *2 x 500 ml (18 fl oz) jars*
Preparation & cooking time: *2 hours*

The spices in this chutney make it lovely and warm with a sort of Mexican feel to it. I've used it in quesadillas made with Stilton, fresh pears and rocket. Fantastic.

2 kg (4 lb 8 oz) ripe plum tomatoes
4 tablespoons vegetable oil
2 teaspoons brown or black mustard seeds
2 teaspoons onion seeds
2 teaspoons fennel seeds
2 teaspoons cumin seeds
2 teaspoons coriander seeds
4 dried red Kashmiri chillies
1 onion, roughly chopped
300 g (10 oz) golden caster sugar
1 litre (1¾ pints) distilled white vinegar
salt to taste

1 Prepare the tomatoes by cutting into quarters and removing the cores.

2 Heat the oil in a large pan or preserving pan and add the seeds and whole chillies. Cook for a minute or two until the seeds start popping. Add the onion, sugar, vinegar and tomatoes. Bring slowly to the boil, stirring often until the sugar has completely dissolved.

3 Cook for about 1 hour, then pick out as many tomato skins as you can (use a pair of long-handled tongs, if you have them).

4 Continue to cook for a further 30 minutes. Check if the chutney is ready by dragging a channel through the mixture (with a wooden spoon) so that the bottom of the pan is visible. If the channel fills immediately with liquid, the chutney is not yet ready. Cook for a further 10 minutes and check again. The chutney is ready when the channel does not fill and the mixture is very thick. Add salt, to taste.

5 Remove the pan from the heat and leave to stand briefly. Carefully pour into hot sterilised jars (page 9) and seal. Allow the chutney to cool completely before labelling and storing in a cool, dark cupboard. Store for at least 2 months before eating.

Indian-spiced Tomato and Pepper Chutney

Makes: *2 x 500 ml (18 fl oz) jars*
Preparation & cooking time: *2 hours*

Although you can use vine tomatoes for this and other tomato recipes, I've found that plum tomatoes have far less water, which means that they cook down more quickly and also produce a higher yield.

2 kg (4 lb 8 oz) ripe plum tomatoes
1 teaspoon black or brown mustard seeds
2 teaspoons cumin seeds
2 teaspoons coriander seeds
1 teaspoon ground turmeric
2 red peppers, de-seeded, quartered and
  sliced thinly crosswise
1 onion, roughly chopped
2 dried red Kashmiri chillies, roughly chopped
2.5 cm (1 inch) piece fresh ginger, peeled
  and grated
300 g (10 oz) golden caster sugar
1 litre (1½ pints) white wine vinegar
salt to taste

1 Prepare the tomatoes by cutting into quarters and removing the cores. Set aside.

2 Heat a small frying pan over a medium heat. Add the seeds and dry-fry for a minute or two, stirring, until the seeds begin to pop. Remove from the heat to a pestle and mortar and grind well. Add the turmeric and set aside.

3 Put the tomatoes, peppers, onion, ground spices, chillies, ginger, sugar and wine vinegar into a large pan or preserving pan. Bring slowly to the boil, stirring often, until all the sugar has dissolved.

4 Cook for about 1 hour, then pick out as many tomato skins as you can (use a pair of long-handled tongs, if you have them).

5 Continue to cook for a further 30 minutes. Check if the chutney is ready by dragging a channel through the mixture (with a wooden spoon) so that the bottom of the pan is visible. If the channel fills immediately with liquid, the chutney is not yet ready. Cook for a further 10 minutes and check again. The chutney is ready when the channel does not fill and the mixture is very thick.

6 Remove the pan from the heat and leave to stand briefly. Add salt to taste. Carefully pour into hot sterilised jars (page 9) and seal. Allow the chutney to cool completely before labelling and storing in a cool, dark cupboard. Store for at least 2 months before eating.

Sweetcorn and Red Pepper Relish

Makes: *1 x 500 ml (18 fl oz) jar*
Preparation & cooking time: *25 minutes*

I love this on a home-made barbecued hamburger on a hot summer night.

1 tablespoon vegetable oil

2 jalapeño or other green chillies, de-seeded and finely chopped

1 red pepper, de-seeded and cut into small dice

1 small red or sweet white onion, finely chopped

1 clove garlic, finely chopped

4 ears fresh sweetcorn, kernels removed from the cob (or 350 g/12 oz frozen sweetcorn)

100 g (3½ oz) granulated sugar (less if you prefer a less sweet relish)

juice of 2 limes

100 ml (3½ fl oz) water

1 tablespoon cornflour

3 tablespoons fresh coriander, chopped, or more to taste

1 teaspoon salt

1 In a large pan or preserving pan, heat the oil over a medium heat. Add the chillies, red pepper, onion and garlic and cook gently until softened, about 5–7 minutes. Add the sweetcorn kernels, sugar, lime juice and water. Bring slowly to the boil, stirring to dissolve the sugar completely. Simmer for about 7–8 minutes, until the sweetcorn is tender.

2 Meanwhile, mix together the cornflour and a little water. Add to the saucepan, stirring constantly, and return to the boil for a further 2 minutes.

3 Stir the coriander and salt into the mixture and remove from the heat. Allow to cool briefly before pouring into hot sterilized jars (page 9) and sealing. Allow the relish to cool completely before labelling. The relish is ready to eat the next day, but can be stored, sealed, for up to 6 months. Once open, eat within a week.

Cranberry and Apple Relish

Makes: *1 x 225 ml (8 fl oz) jar*
Preparation & cooking time: *20 minutes*

400 g (14 oz) cranberries, fresh or frozen
200 g (7 oz) Granny Smith apples, cored and
    finely chopped
50 g (2 oz) raisins
1 tablespoon finely chopped preserved ginger
    (page 116)
75 ml (3 fl oz) white wine vinegar
75 g (2½ oz) caster sugar
large pinch chilli flakes
pinch ground allspice
pinch freshly ground black pepper
50 g (2 oz) redcurrant jelly (page 38)

1 Put all the ingredients, except the redcurrant
jelly, into a large pan or preserving pan and
bring slowly to the boil, stirring often until
the sugar has completely dissolved. Simmer
for 10 minutes, until the cranberries are just
beginning to burst.

2 Remove from the heat and stir in the
redcurrant jelly until completely dissolved.
Allow the mixture to cool briefly before pouring
into hot sterilized jars (page 9) and sealing.
Allow the relish to cool completely before
labelling. The relish is ready to eat the next
day, but can be stored, sealed, for up to 6
months. Once open, eat within a week.

Ratatouille Relish

Makes: *2 x 500 ml (18 fl oz) jars*
Preparation & cooking time: *45 minutes*

2 tablespoons olive oil
1 large courgette, cut into small dice
1 large red pepper, cut into small dice
1 medium aubergine, cut into small dice
1 large red onion, finely chopped
500 g (1lb 2 oz) ripe tomatoes, skinned and
    roughly chopped
1 clove garlic, crushed
1 tablespoon fresh thyme leaves
pinch chilli flakes
100 g (3½ oz) caster sugar
200 ml (7 fl oz) red wine vinegar

1 Heat the oil over a medium heat in a large pan
or preserving pan. Add the courgette, pepper,
aubergine and onion. Increase the heat and
cook, stirring, until the vegetables are soft and
just starting to take on some colour – about
8–10 minutes.

2 Add the tomatoes, garlic, thyme, chilli flakes,
sugar and red wine vinegar. Bring slowly to the
boil, stirring often until the sugar has dissolved
completely.

3 Simmer for about 20 minutes until the mixture
has thickened. Remove from the heat. Allow to
cool briefly before pouring into hot sterilized jars
(page 9) and sealing. Allow to cool completely
before labelling. The relish is ready to eat the
next day, but can be stored, sealed, for up to 6
months. Once open, eat within a week.

Cucumber Relish

Makes: *3 x 500 ml (18 fl oz) jars*
Preparation & cooking time: *1½ hours*

This is the kind of relish that was an essential addition to hamburgers and hot dogs when I was a child. Okay, so it still is … My mother always bought a commercially prepared relish, but only because she never tried this recipe.

3 large cucumbers
300 g (10½ oz) carrots, grated
2 large onions, grated
1 large green pepper, de-seeded and
   finely diced
1 tablespoon salt
300 g (10½ oz) caster sugar
1 litre (1¾ pints) distilled white vinegar
1 teaspoon mustard seeds
1 teaspoon celery seeds
1 teaspoon ground turmeric
5 tablespoons cornflour

1 To prepare the cucumbers, halve them crosswise then again lengthwise to give four pieces. Using a teaspoon, scoop out the seeds. Grate the cucumbers coarsely or cut into very fine dice if you prefer (or have time).

2 Put the prepared cucumbers, carrots, onions and green pepper into a large colander. Sprinkle with the salt and set aside in the sink for 30 minutes. Rinse well, then pat dry on kitchen paper.

3 Transfer to a large pan or preserving pan along with the sugar, vinegar, mustard and celery seeds and turmeric. Bring to the boil, stirring often until the sugar has dissolved. Simmer gently for 30 minutes.

4 Mix the cornflour with 5 tablespoons of water. Add this to the pan, stirring well. Simmer for a further 5 minutes until thickened. Allow the relish to cool briefly before pouring into hot sterilized jars (page 9) and sealing. Allow it to cool completely before labelling. The relish is ready to eat the next day, but can be stored, sealed, for up to 6 months. Once open, eat within a week.

Tomato Relish

Makes: *3 x 500 ml (18 fl oz) jars*
Preparation & cooking time: *1¾ hours*

I find this relish a great accompaniment to cheese but try it spooned on to a sausage too.

1.75 kg (4 lb) firm ripe plum tomatoes, skinned
  and roughly chopped
1 kg (2 lb 4 oz) onions, finely chopped
1 garlic clove, crushed
½ teaspoon chilli flakes
1 teaspoon mustard seeds
1 teaspoon ground ginger
1 tablespoon chilli powder
1 teaspoon salt
750 g (1lb 10 oz) caster sugar
100 g (3½ oz) light brown soft sugar
450 ml (16 fl oz) malt vinegar
salt, to taste

1 Put all the ingredients, except the sugars, vinegar and salt, into a large pan or preserving pan. Bring slowly to the boil and simmer gently, uncovered, for about 1 hour, until the mixture thickens. Add the sugars and vinegar and cook for a further 20 minutes until thickened. Add salt to taste.

2 Allow the relish to cool briefly before pouring into hot sterilized jars (page 9) and sealing. Allow it to cool completely before labelling. The relish is ready to eat the next day, but can be stored, sealed, for up to 6 months. Once open, eat within a week.

Courgette Relish

Makes: *2 x 500 ml (18 fl oz) jars*
Preparation & cooking time: *45 minutes + standing overnight*

It's very important to rinse the vegetables thoroughly to remove the excess salt. If you are not thorough in patting them dry, you will need to cook the relish for longer to boil off the excess water.

1 kg (2 lb 4 oz) courgettes, finely grated
2 large onions, finely grated
2 red peppers, finely sliced
5 tablespoons salt
1 litre (1¾ pints) white wine vinegar
2 tablespoons ground turmeric
300 g (10½ oz) caster sugar
1 tablespoon mustard powder
1 tablespoon cornflour
1 tablespoon black peppercorns
2 tablespoons celery seeds

1 Put the courgettes, onions and red peppers into a large bowl and sprinkle with the salt. Cover and leave to stand overnight. Rinse and drain well then pat dry on kitchen paper.

2 Put the vegetables and remaining ingredients into a large pan or preserving pan and bring slowly to the boil, stirring often until the sugar has dissolved completely. Simmer gently for about 20 minutes.

3 Remove the pan from the heat. Allow the relish to cool briefly before pouring into hot sterilized jars (page 9) and sealing. Allow it to cool completely before labelling. The relish is ready to eat the next day, but can be stored sealed for up to 6 months. Once open, eat within a week.

Chilli Jam

Makes: *1 x 300 ml (10 fl oz) jar*
Preparation & cooking time: *50 minutes*

This fiery preserve was the invention of some innovative chefs in the late 1990s. The addition of vinegar makes it more of a relish than a jam, and it is definitely best accompanying savoury dishes – I wouldn't recommend spreading it on your morning toast! Not all chillies are created equal, at least as far as heat is concerned, so you may want to adjust the quantity of chillies to your taste.

500 g (1 lb 2 oz) very ripe tomatoes, roughly chopped
4 red finger chillies, de-seeded (optional) and roughly chopped
2 cloves garlic, roughly chopped
2.5 cm (1 inch) piece fresh ginger, peeled and roughly chopped
1 tablespoon Thai fish sauce
225 g (8 oz) soft brown sugar
3 tablespoons red wine vinegar

1 Put half the tomatoes into a blender, along with the chillies, garlic, ginger and fish sauce. Whizz everything to a fine purée and pour the mixture into a large pan or preserving pan along with the sugar and vinegar. Slowly bring the mixture up to boiling point, stirring all the time until the sugar has dissolved.

2 Pulse the remaining tomatoes until they are a chunky pulp and add this to the pan. Return to the boil and reduce to a simmer.

3 Skim off any foam from the surface and cook gently, uncovered, for 30–40 minutes, stirring every 5 minutes to prevent the chopped tomatoes settling at the bottom. You will also need to scrape down the sides of the pan during the cooking so that everything cooks evenly. The mixture should reduce to half its volume. Test for a set (page 12). If necessary, boil for a further 5 minutes before testing again. Continue testing at 5-minute intervals, as necessary, until the jam has reached setting point.

4 Remove from the heat, skim off any scum and allow the jam to cool briefly. Carefully pour into hot sterilised jars (page 9). Seal the jars and allow the jam to cool completely before labelling and storing.

Pickles

Pickling usually involves brining and/or steeping in vinegar. The brine draws out excess water from the vegetables and ensures they remain crisp once pickled in vinegar. Some vegetables, if they contain sufficient water, can be pickled using only salt – for example, Sauerkraut uses this method. In this chapter you'll find all the favourites – Pickled Onions, Bread and Butter Pickles and Sweet Pickled Beetroot – alongside some interesting twists. Try Dill Courgette Pickles, Pickled Garlic or Warm Spiced Pickled Pears – an excellent accompaniment to cold meat.

Bread and Butter Pickles

Makes: *2 x 500 ml (18 fl oz) jars*
Preparation & cooking time: *30 minutes +
3 hours standing*

**6 large cucumbers (about 800 g/1 lb 11 oz),
    thinly sliced**
4 onions, thinly sliced
50 g (2 oz) table salt
450 ml (16 fl oz) distilled vinegar
175 g (6 oz) granulated sugar
½ teaspoon ground turmeric
1 teaspoon celery seeds
1 teaspoon mustard seeds

1 Mix together the cucumbers, onions, salt and
lots of roughly crushed ice in a large bowl.
Mix well. Put a weight on top – a plate topped
with a couple of cans will do – and allow the
mixture to stand for 3 hours. Drain thoroughly.

2 Combine the vinegar, sugar, turmeric,
celery and mustard seeds in a large pan or
preserving pan. Add the drained cucumbers
and onions.

3 Place the pan on a medium-low heat and
bring to the point of boiling, but DO NOT
ALLOW TO BOIL. Remove immediately from
the heat.

4 Allow to cool briefly before pouring into hot
sterilized jars (page 9) and sealing. Allow to
cool completely before labelling. The pickles
are ready to eat the next day but will improve
if left sealed for 2 weeks. Once opened, eat
within 2 weeks. Sealed, these pickles will keep
for up to a year.

Pickled Garlic

Makes: *1 x 500 ml (18 fl oz) jar*
Preparation & cooking time: *30 minutes*

If you prefer, make this recipe
in the spring when fresh garlic
is available (the heads of garlic
with green stems attached).
Simply peel the coarsest outer
layers of papery skin away
and pickle the heads whole.
Use in Thai recipes or serve as
a pickle, as you would serve
pickled onions or cucumbers.

**8 heads of garlic, separated into individual
    cloves and, I'm sorry to say, peeled**
225 ml (8 fl oz) red wine vinegar
900 ml (1½ pints) water
175 g (6 oz) granulated sugar
1 tablespoon salt
2 small dried hot chillies
8 cloves
2 teaspoons black peppercorns

1 Place all the ingredients in a large pan or
preserving pan. Bring to the boil and simmer
gently for 10 minutes, stirring from time to time.

2 Remove from the heat and leave to cool to
room temperature. Transfer to a cold sterilised
jar (page 9). Seal and store for at least
1 month before serving.

Dill Courgette Pickles

Makes: *2 x 1 litre (1¾ pint) jars*
Preparation & cooking time: *20 minutes + 2 hours standing*

Feel free to substitute pickling cucumbers in this recipe, but do try the pickled courgettes – they are unusually good.

8 medium courgettes, each about 20 cm
   (8 inches), or as tall as your jars
75 g (3 oz) pickling or coarse salt
750 ml (1¼ pints) distilled white vinegar
750 g (1½ lb) caster sugar
500 ml (18 fl oz) water
1 tablespoon mustard seeds
2 teaspoons celery seeds
2 cloves garlic, peeled and left whole (one for
   each jar)
2 sprigs dill

1 Trim the courgettes and cut them in half lengthwise. Place in a large bowl and add the salt. Cover with water and leave to stand for 2 hours. Drain well.

2 In a large pan or preserving pan, mix together the vinegar, sugar, water, mustard and celery seeds. Bring to boil, reduce the heat and simmer for 5 minutes.

3 Meanwhile, put one clove of garlic in the bottom of each hot sterilised jar. Carefully stand the courgettes in the jars, fitting them in very snugly. Add the dill sprigs on top. Pour in the hot liquid to cover, leaving 1 cm (½ inch) space at the top. Seal and label the jars when cold. Leave to stand for 1 week before using. Store for up to 1 year.

Pickled Onions

Makes: *3 x 500 ml (18 fl oz) jars*
Preparation & cooking time: *30 minutes + standing overnight*

If you prefer the onions to be softer, add the spiced vinegar when still hot – making sure the jars are also hot or they will crack.

250 g (9 oz) rock salt
2 litres (3½ pints) water
1.5 kg (3 lb 5 oz) shallots or small pickling
   onions, peeled and trimmed
1 litre (1¾ pints) malt vinegar
1 tablespoon each allspice berries,
   juniper berries, black peppercorns
   and mustard seeds
1 cinnamon stick
2 bay leaves
100 g (3½ oz) light muscovado sugar

1 Put the salt and water into a large saucepan, dissolve the salt over a low heat and then leave the brine to cool. Add the prepared shallots or onions, weigh down with a plate topped with a couple of cans and leave in a cool place for 24 hours.

2 The next day, put the vinegar and all the spices and sugar into a large pan or preserving pan and bring to the boil, stirring until the sugar is dissolved. Remove from the heat and leave until cold.

3 Drain the shallots or onions and carefully pack into cold sterilised jars (page 9). Pour over the infused vinegar and the spices. Seal, label and leave in a cool dark place for 3–4 weeks before eating.

Sweet Pickled Beetroot

Makes: *2 x 500 ml (18 fl oz) jars*
Preparation & cooking time: *2¼ hours*

Unless you like your hands a bright shade of pink, I would handle the cooked beetroot with rubber gloves!

1 litre (1¾ pints) white wine vinegar
1 teaspoon salt
½ cinnamon stick
4 black peppercorns
4 whole cloves
225 g (8 oz) caster sugar
1 kg (2 lb 4 oz) small raw beetroot, washed and tops trimmed but not peeled

1 Place the vinegar, salt, cinnamon, peppercorns, cloves and sugar in a large pan or preserving pan. Bring to the boil and cook, stirring, until the sugar has dissolved.

2 Add the whole beets, then cover and simmer for 1½–2 hours, depending on the size of beetroot used, until they are completely tender. Do not break the skins or they will lose their colour. Remove the pan from the heat and leave to cool.

3 Remove the beets from the cooking liquid with a slotted spoon, then peel (the skins will practically rub off) and either dice or slice thickly, as you prefer. If the beets are very small, you could leave them whole. Pack into sterilized jars to within 2.5 cm (1 inch) from the tops.

4 Reheat the vinegar mixture in the pan until boiling, then carefully strain over the beetroot until well covered.

5 Tap the jars to remove air pockets then seal. Label when cold and store in a cool, dark place for at least 3 weeks before eating.

Pickled Gherkins

Makes: *4 x 500 ml (18 fl oz) jars*
Preparation & cooking time: *10 minutes + 4 days standing*

2 litres (3½ pints) water
200 g (7 oz) pickling or rock salt
2 kg (4 lb 8 oz) small pickling cucumbers
 or gherkins
4 cloves garlic, peeled and chopped
2 tablespoons freshly chopped dill
1.5 litres (2½ pints) white distilled vinegar

1 Stir together the water and salt until the salt
 has completely dissolved. Wash the gherkins
 then place in a large non-metallic bowl. Pour
 over the brine. Cover and leave for 3 days.
 Drain well then pack the gherkins into hot
 sterilised jars (page 9) along with the garlic
 and dill.

2 Put the vinegar into a large pan and bring
 to the boil. Pour into the jars to cover the
 gherkins. Leave for 24 hours.

3 Pour off the vinegar into a large pan, and once
 again bring to the boil. Pour back into the jars
 (the gherkins should turn bright green). Ensure
 that the gherkins are completely covered by
 the vinegar.

4 Seal and label when cold. The gherkins
 are ready to eat the next day, but will keep,
 sealed, for 6 months. Refrigerate once
 opened and use within 1 month.

Orange Pickle

Makes: *1 x 500 ml (18 fl oz) jar*
Preparation & cooking time: *2 hours*

1 cinnamon stick
1 teaspoon whole cloves
1 strip lemon zest
700 ml (1¼ pints) white wine vinegar
450 g (1 lb) caster sugar
6 oranges (about 1 kg/2 lb 4 oz)

1 Put the cinnamon, cloves and lemon zest into
 a muslin square and tie up to make a small
 bag. Set aside.

2 Put the vinegar and sugar into a large pan or
 preserving pan. Add the spices in their small
 bag and bring to the boil, stirring often, until
 the sugar has dissolved.

3 Meanwhile, peel the oranges, removing all the
 pith. Slice the flesh thickly and remove any
 pips. Add the sliced oranges to the pan and
 return to the boil. Simmer gently for about
 1–1½ hours. Remove from the heat and take
 out the muslin bag.

4 Allow the mixture to cool for 20 minutes
 before pouring into hot sterilized jars (page
 9). Allow the pickle to cool completely before
 labelling the jars.

Chilli-lilli

Makes: *4 x 500 ml (18 fl oz) jars*
Preparation & cooking time: *50 minutes + salting overnight*

This recipe makes a nice change from the standard piccalilli, but leave out the chilli if you like yours the old-fashioned way.

2.7 kg (6 lb) vegetables – include cauliflower, baby onions, cucumber, baby green tomatoes, runner beans
4 (or more, to taste) red finger chillies, de-seeded and sliced thickly
200 g (7 oz) salt
1.2 litres (2 pints) white distilled vinegar
175 g (6 oz) caster sugar
25 g (1 oz) dry mustard powder
25g (1 oz) ground ginger
15 g (½ oz) ground turmeric
40 g (1½ oz) cornflour or plain flour

1 Wash and prepare the vegetables: cut into roughly equal-sized pieces – around 3 cm (1¼ inches). Spread the vegetables and chillies over a large dish and sprinkle with the salt. Place a plate on top to weigh them down and leave in a cool place for 24 hours. Drain, wash and rinse the vegetables.

2 Put 1 litre (1¾ pints) of the vinegar and the sugar and spices into a large pan or preserving pan and heat gently until the sugar has dissolved. Add the vegetables and chillies, return to the boil and simmer gently for 5 minutes, or until just tender (the vegetables will continue to soften during pickling so don't overcook).

3 Meanwhile, whisk the cornflour or flour with the remaining vinegar until smooth, then add to the vegetables in the pan. Bring to the boil and simmer gently for a further 2–3 minutes until thickened.

4 Remove from the heat and leave to stand briefly. Carefully pour into hot sterilised jars (page 9) and seal. Allow the pickle to cool completely before labelling. Store the chilli-lilli in a cool, dark cupboard for at least 6 weeks before eating.

Warm Spiced Pickled Pears

Makes: *4 x 500 ml (18 fl oz) jars*
Preparation & cooking time: *40 minutes*

The spices are warm, not the pears! An excellent and unusual accompaniment to cold meats, try these pears with roast duck or goose.

10 allspice berries
6 whole cloves
½ cinnamon stick
1 teaspoon mixed peppercorns
1 star anise
zest of 1 unwaxed lemon, peeled into
　　large strips
a thumb-sized piece of fresh ginger, peeled
　　and sliced
350 ml (12 fl oz) white wine vinegar
300 ml (10 fl oz) cider vinegar
350 g (12 oz) light brown soft sugar
1.5 kg (3 lb 5 oz) firm unblemished pears

1　Put all the ingredients, apart from the pears, into a large pan or preserving pan. Bring slowly to the boil, stirring occasionally, until the sugar has dissolved.

2　Meanwhile, peel the pears, leaving the stem intact – there's no need to core them either – and place in a large bowl of cold water to stop them from discolouring. When the spice mixture comes to the boil, add the pears. Top up the pan with hot water to cover the pears if necessary.

3　Simmer gently for about 15–20 minutes until the flesh of the pears looks slightly translucent and the tip of a sharp knife inserted into a pear meets no resistance.

4　Remove the pears from the pan to sterilised jars (page 9), then return the remaining cooking liquid to a fast boil until reduced down to about 1 litre (1¾ pints). Pour the hot syrup over the pears (discard any syrup you don't need), add the whole spices and seal. Label when cold and store for up to 6 months.

Sauerkraut

Makes: *3 x 500 ml (18 fl oz) jars*
Preparation & cooking time: *1 hour + 4–6 weeks fermenting*

There's no quick way to make your own sauerkraut. You need to leave yourself up to a month for the cabbage to ferment before it can be cooked and bottled. You will also need a crock-pot of some kind in which to ferment your cabbage – ceramic or food-grade plastic will do – plus a plate that fits inside it to weight the cabbage (a cloth and a few cans will do).

**2.75 kg (6 lb) cabbage (a mix of red and green
    gives a nice pink sauerkraut)
3 tablespoons salt
3 sharp eating apples, e.g. Granny Smith,
    cored and coarsely grated
10 cracked juniper berries**

1 Using a sharp knife or food processor with a slicing blade, shred the cabbage and mix it with the salt – the salt draws water from the cabbage and creates the brine in which it ferments and sours without rotting. Stir in the apples and cracked juniper berries.

2 Put the mixture into the clean pot, leaving at least 5 cm (2 inches) at the top. Cover with a clean, wet, preferably linen, cloth and place the plate on top. Put the weights on top of the plate. This will force the brine to rise high enough to reach the cloth. If, after 24 hours, this hasn't happened, make brine by dissolving 1 tablespoon of salt in 1 litre (1¾ pints) water and add enough of this to cover the cabbage (some cabbage, particularly in winter, simply has less water).

3 Leave the sauerkraut in a cool place indoors to ferment, but skim off any scum from the surface every other day. Replace the damp cloth frequently. At 16°C (60°F), the fermenting process will take at least a month. To check, taste the sauerkraut at regular intervals until it has developed a sourness that is pleasing to you. A higher temperature will speed up the process, but the flavour will not be as good, so it is best to leave your sauerkraut in a cool cellar or larder or an unheated room.

4 Once fermentation is finished and you are happy with the flavour of your sauerkraut, place the cabbage mixture in a large pan or preserving pan and bring to the boil over a medium heat. Remove from the heat and ladle the hot sauerkraut into hot sterilised jars (page 9). Leave until cold then label before storing for up to 12 months.

Note: Sauerkraut can be eaten cold, but it's more often warmed up. A traditional serving suggestion is to heat it with pieces of bacon and a liberal dollop of goose fat. It is also good with just about any pork dish.

Mostarda di Cremona
(fruits preserved in mustard syrup)

Makes: *1 x l litre (1¾ pints) jar or 2 x 600 ml (1 pint) jars*
Preparation & cooking time: *2½ hours + 3 days macerating*

I leave the choice of fruit up to you. Traditionally, mostarda is made with quinces or grapes, but other fruits work very well, especially in combination, including pears, apples, cherries, figs, plums, peaches and tangerines. As for using mostarda di cremona, it is traditional to serve it with bollito misto, an Italian dish of boiled meats, but it is excellent with cold meats and cheese too. It is also an unusual addition to pumpkin-filled ravioli. The high sugar content of this preserve means that heat-sealing is unnecessary to prevent spoilage.

2 kg (4 lb 8 oz) peeled, cored and cleaned fruit
   (such as grapes, pears, plums, quinces
   – see above)
1 kg (2 lb 4 oz) caster sugar (or half the weight
   of the fruit)
50 g (2 oz) dry mustard powder
1 teaspoon yellow mustard seeds
1 teaspoon chilli flakes
1 glass dry white wine

1 You can leave small fruits such as grapes whole, but larger fruit should be halved or quartered.

1 In a large bowl, mix together the prepared fruit and sugar. Cover and allow the mixture to sit in the refrigerator for 24 hours.

2 Strain the juices from the fruit over a medium-sized pan or preserving pan. Return the fruit to the bowl. Bring the sugar mixture to the boil and simmer for about 30 minutes or until reduced and syrupy. Keep an eye on it – you don't want to end up with a caramel, just a thick syrup.

3 Pour the hot syrup over the fruit in the bowl. Leave uncovered at room temperature for a further 24 hours.

4 Strain the fruit again over a medium saucepan. The syrup will have drawn additional moisture from the fruit, so it will be thinner than it was the day before. Repeat step 2, reducing the liquid to a thick syrup again. Pour the hot syrup over the fruit and let it sit for another 24 hours, again uncovered.

5 Repeat the straining and reducing as on the third day. Meanwhile, prepare the mustard flavouring. In a small saucepan mix the mustard powder, mustard seeds and chilli flakes with a glass of white wine. Bring to the boil. Allow to reduce by one third.

6 Sterilize 2 x 600 ml (1 pint) jars (page 9). Carefully fill the two jars with the fruit. Divide the reduced mustard-wine syrup equally between the jars. Finally, cover the fruit with the syrup to the top, discarding any excess. Tap the jars a few times while filling with the syrup to remove any air bubbles. Press the fruit down and close. Allow the syrup to cool before labelling and storing. Leave to sit, undisturbed, for at least 2 weeks before using.

Note: The weight of fruit given should fill a 1 litre (1¾ pint) jar about one and a half times, as the fruit will shrink during the preparation. Adjust quantities as necessary to fill your jar one and a half times.

Lemon and Lime Pickle

Makes: *1 x 750 g (1 lb 10 oz) jar*
Preparation & cooking time: *2½ hours*

Traditionally, this pickle would be made by mixing everything together in a large glass jar and then leaving it in the heat of the sun to 'cook'. If you have a sunny, south-facing windowsill and want to try making it that way, put the jar in the sunniest possible position (consider moving it around if you have to) and leave it for about 2 months or until the citrus skins have softened completely. In this case, it is best made around May/June. Alternatively, make it using the following method, though the flavour will be less vivid.

4 lemons
2 limes
75 g (3 oz) salt
65 g (2½ oz) sugar
2 teaspoons cayenne (or more, to taste)
1 tablespoon ground turmeric
1 teaspoon methi seeds
1 teaspoon black mustard seeds
¼ teaspoon asafoetida powder

1 To prepare the fruit, remove the stem end of each fruit and chop into bite-sized pieces. Put into a large pan or preserving pan along with the salt and sugar. Add 50 ml (2 fl oz) water and bring the mixture slowly to the boil, stirring often until the sugar and salt have dissolved completely.

2 Meanwhile, put the spices, powdered and whole, into a dry frying pan over a medium heat and cook for 2–3 minutes until the whole spices begin to pop and the whole mixture darkens by a shade – it will also smell very fragrant.

3 Transfer the spices to a mortar and grind with a pestle until fine (or use a spice grinder or coffee grinder). Add the ground spices to the fruit pan and stir well.

4 Simmer the mixture gently until the fruit is very soft, about 1½–2 hours. Remove from the heat. Allow to cool for 20 minutes before pouring into the hot sterilized jar. Allow to cool completely before labelling. Store for at least 2 months before using.

Preserved Lemons

Makes: *1 x 1 litre (1¾ pints) jar*
Preparation & cooking time: *10 minutes*

Traditionally, lemons are preserved only in salt but here I have offered the option of adding a few flavouring ingredients to the jar – perfect if you are giving them as a gift.

4–6 lemons (depending on the size of your jar)
75 g (3 oz) coarse sea salt
2 bay leaves (optional)
2 cinnamon sticks, broken in half (optional)
4 cloves (optional)
3–4 extra lemons, for juicing

1 Clean and sterilise a jar. Approximately 1 litre (1¾ pints) will hold 4–6 lemons – make sure they are tightly packed.

2 Cut the lemons into quarters, leaving the quarters attached at the base (so that they open up but don't separate). Pack one of the cut lemons with some of the salt and put into the jar. Repeat with the remaining lemons and salt, adding all the salt to the jar. Add the bay leaves, cinnamon and cloves as you go.

3 Squeeze the juice from three or four additional lemons and add this to the jar also. Press everything down and add water to cover the lemons. Seal the jar and set aside for approximately 1 month, until the lemons have softened – their colour will change from bright yellow to soft, murky yellow. Keep for up to a year.

Compôtes, Candies and Dried Fruit

Compôtes are not strictly preserves (though they will keep for several weeks if packed, hot, into sterilised jars), but they are an excellent way to use up a glut of fruit. Good with ice cream or a plain sponge, try compôtes cold, folded through Greek yoghurt, or use them as a base for fools, mixed with custard and softly whipped cream. Candying fruit is a simple but time-consuming process. The method described here for citrus peel is very effective and the result is the freshest candied peel you'll ever taste. Home-dried fruit is also easy. You'll end up with fruit that is less leathery than commercially dried products, with a freshness you can't buy.

Spiced Dried Fruit Compôte

Makes: *2 x 500 ml (18 fl oz) jars*
Preparation & cooking time: *45 minutes*

In this recipe, fresh and dried fruit is cooked slowly in spiced sugar syrup. The slow cooking ensures that the fruit retains its shape.

1 cinnamon stick
4 cloves
1 pared strip lemon zest
150 g (5 oz) light brown soft sugar
200 g (7 oz) dried figs
200 g (7 oz) dried apricots
200 g (7 oz) prunes
200 g (7 oz) dried peaches
2 medium size firm pears, peeled, cored and
   cut into sixths lengthwise

1 Put the cinnamon, cloves, lemon zest and sugar into a medium saucepan along with 300 ml (½ pint) water. Bring slowly to the boil, stirring often until all the sugar has dissolved. Boil for 4 minutes until syrupy. Add the dried fruit and return to a gentle simmer.

2 Cook gently for 15 minutes before adding the pears. Return again to a gentle simmer and cook for a further 15 minutes until the pears are tender, all the dried fruit has plumped up and the syrup is quick thick.

3 Transfer to a clean jar or airtight container and keep in the refrigerator for up to 1 week. Serve warm or cold with cream, ice cream or Greek yoghurt.

Raspberry Compôte

Makes: *1 x 500 ml (18 fl oz) jar*
Preparation & cooking time: *10 minutes*

This really couldn't be simpler. Serve with just about any cream-based dessert, but this compôte really suits white and dark chocolate too.

500 g (1 lb 2 oz) raspberries
100 g (3½ oz) caster sugar
juice of 1 lemon

1 Put the raspberries, sugar and lemon juice into a medium saucepan over a medium-low heat. Stir gently to dissolve the sugar.

2 As soon as the mixture begins to boil, reduce the heat and cook for 3–4 minutes until the raspberry juices begin to run. Remove from the heat.

3 Transfer to a clean jar or airtight container and keep in the refrigerator for up to 1 week.

Plum Compôte

Makes: *2 x 500 ml (18 fl oz) jars*
Preparation & cooking time: *20 minutes*

Use this delicious compôte as the basis for a crumble, or serve on its own, warm or cold, with cream or ice cream.

50 g (2 oz) butter
1.5 kg (3 lb 5 oz) fresh dark plums, halved,
    stones removed
1 vanilla pod, split in half lengthwise
1 star anise
pinch nutmeg, freshly grated
2 cinnamon sticks
100 ml (3½ fl oz) red wine
5 tablespoons golden syrup
4 tablespoons caster sugar

1 Melt the butter in a medium saucepan and add the plums. Fry for 2–3 minutes until starting to soften then add the vanilla pod, star anise, nutmeg and cinnamon sticks. Stir until the spices become fragrant then add the red wine, golden syrup and sugar. Stir briefly until the sugar has dissolved.

2 Bring to a simmer and cook for 8–10 minutes, stirring often, until the plums have broken down to a thick sauce. Remove the whole spices.

3 Transfer the compôte to a clean jar or airtight container and keep in the refrigerator for up to 1 week.

Strawberry Vanilla Compôte

Makes: *1 x 500 ml (18 fl oz) jars*
Preparation & cooking time: *10 minutes*

The whole fruits in this compôte mean that it not only tastes beautiful, it is also stunning to look at.

500 g (1 lb 2 oz) strawberries, washed and
   hulled, large fruit cut in half
150 g (5 oz) caster sugar
juice of ½ lemon
1 vanilla pod, split lengthwise

1 Put all the ingredients into a medium saucepan over a medium-low heat. Stir gently to dissolve the sugar.

2 When the mixture begins to boil, reduce the heat to low, cover and cook gently for 4–5 minutes, until the fruit is soft and the juices are quite syrupy. Remove from the heat. Remove the vanilla pod.

3 Transfer to a clean jar or airtight container and keep in the refrigerator for up to 1 week. Serve warm or cold with cream, ice cream or Greek yoghurt.

Candied Peel

Makes: *1 x 500 ml (18 fl oz) jar*
Preparation & cooking time: *4 hours + 3–4 days drying*

Although it is now possible to buy very good quality candied peel, nothing beats the fresh taste of home made. Although it is a bit time consuming, it's not difficult to do and it will transform anything you use it in. Use unwaxed fruit, when available. Because limes don't tend to have a great deal of pith, avoid using them in this recipe as it is the thick pith that makes the candied peel succulent.

2 lemons, preferably unwaxed
2 oranges, preferably unwaxed
1 pink or ruby grapefruit
1 pomelo
600 g (1 lb 5 oz) granulated sugar
caster sugar, for coating

1 If you're using waxed fruit, scrub it thoroughly under hot running water with a drop of washing-up liquid. Slice off the top and bottom of each fruit then cut the peel in wide strips, from top to bottom, making sure that the pith remains attached to the skin. Place each variety of peel in a separate pan, fill with cold water and boil until soft. Depending on the fruit, this can take up to 90 minutes. Keep the water replenished with a freshly boiled kettle.

2 Drain and place all the peel in one saucepan. Cover with cold water, bring to the boil and cook for a further 20 minutes before draining.

3 Meanwhile, dissolve the sugar in 300 ml (½ pint) water in a large, thick-bottomed saucepan over a low heat. Bring to the boil and gently stir in the peel. Reduce the heat and simmer gently, stirring occasionally, until the peel has absorbed nearly all the syrup. You should allow 2–3 hours for this. Keep an eye on the pan towards the end of the cooking time to prevent the peel from sticking to the bottom.

4 Lightly oil a grill rack and line it with greaseproof paper. Arrange the peel in a single layer on the rack. If possible, put in a warm place, like an airing cupboard. Allow 3–4 days to dry, turning the peel over twice during this time, to allow both sides to dry. It will be very sticky.

5 Put some caster sugar into a bowl and add a few pieces of peel at a time. Turn them gently in the sugar until coated. Repeat with all the peel, adding more caster sugar as necessary. Return the peel to clean greaseproof paper and leave out for another day. Once the peel is dry, store it in an airtight jar. Snip into smaller pieces as and when you need it.

Preserved Ginger

Makes: *2 x 500 ml (18 fl oz) jars*
Preparation & cooking time: *2 hours + soaking overnight*

Use very fresh ginger for this – old, dried or discoloured ginger won't work. If you can, go to an Oriental or Indian supermarket, where the turnover is quite high and the ginger will be in excellent condition.

500 g (1 lb 2 oz) fresh ginger, peeled and scrubbed, cut into 5 cm (2 inch) pieces (turn them into little balls, if you prefer)
500 g (1 lb 2 oz) caster sugar
350 ml (12 fl oz) water

1 Rinse the ginger pieces and place them in a bowl of cold water. Cover and leave overnight. Drain well.

2 Put the ginger into a medium saucepan and cover with cold water. Bring to the boil and simmer for 10 minutes. Drain and repeat, boiling and draining three or more times until the ginger is quite tender – the number of times you need to do this will depend on the freshness of your ginger.

3 In a separate pan, mix together the sugar and the measured water and bring to the boil, stirring often until the sugar is dissolved. Simmer for 20 minutes until quite syrupy. Add the drained ginger and bring once again to the boil. Simmer for 30 minutes, uncovered.

4 Remove the pan from heat and leave to stand briefly then carefully pour into hot sterilised jars (page 9) and seal. Allow the ginger syrup to cool completely before labelling and storing. The preserved ginger keeps for a year, sealed. Use within 3 months once opened.

Home-dried Fruit Apple Rings

Makes: *about 500 g (1 lb 2 oz)*
Preparation & cooking time: *1 hour + 3 hours cooling*

4 medium-sharp eating apples, e.g. Granny
    Smith
juice of 1 lemon
pinch ground cinnamon (optional)

1 Core the apples – peel them if you prefer,
though you don't need to. Slice the apples
into rings about 5 mm (¼ inch) thick.

2 To keep the apple rings from browning too
much, combine about 450 ml (¾ pint) cold
water and the lemon juice in a large bowl. Add
the apple rings, making sure each piece gets
coated with the water-lemon mixture. Leave
to stand for 5 minutes then drain well. Pat the
apple rings dry with kitchen paper.

3 Preheat the oven to Gas Mark ½/130°C/
250°F. Lightly spray two wire racks with
cooking spray or vegetable oil – use a brush
if you don't have an oil sprayer, but be careful
not to use too much oil; a light coating is all
you want. Arrange the apple rings in a single
layer on the wire racks, making sure they
don't touch or overlap. Sprinkle lightly with the
cinnamon, if using. Set each rack on a baking
sheet and transfer to the oven for 30 minutes.

4 Switch the trays if they're on different shelves
and bake for a further 30 minutes. Turn off the
oven but leave the apple rings in for 3 hours or
until cold. Remove from the oven. Store in an
airtight container and use within 2 weeks.

Dried Pineapple Rings

Use a fresh, ripe pineapple. Cut off the base
and green spikes. Remove the skin and eyes.
Slice the pineapple thinly. Lay the slices in a
single layer on a baking tray lined with baking
parchment. Sprinkle lightly with caster sugar.
Bake at Gas Mark 1/140°C/275°F for 2 hours
until dried. Store as for apples.

Dried Pears

In a small saucepan, mix together 50 g
(2 oz) caster sugar, 150 ml (¼ pint) water, a
good squeeze of lemon juice and ½ teaspoon
ground cardamom (or 2–3 cracked cardamom
pods). Stir over a medium heat until the sugar
has dissolved. Increase the heat and boil for 3–4
minutes until syrupy. Set aside. Meanwhile, core
3 medium-sized, ripe but firm pears and slice
thinly. Dip the pear slices in the slightly cooled
syrup and lay in a single layer on baking tray,
lined with baking parchment. Bake in the oven at
Gas Mark 1/140°C/275°F for 2–3 hours until dry
and crisp, changing the trays over once or twice.
Store as for apples.

Sauces and Spreads

In this chapter you'll find a collection of recipes to help you deal with a glut of tomatoes, as well as a collection of quick sauces suitable for midweek suppers. You'll also find some useful spreads for sandwiches and hors d'oeuvres. The tomato sauces don't necessarily need bottling, as they can be eaten straight away, but if you have some tomato plants and suddenly find yourself with armfuls, why not put some up for a midwinter supper of the quickest order?

Redcurrant Sauce

Makes: *2 x 225 ml (8 fl oz) jars*
Preparation & cooking time: *30 minutes*

This slightly sweet, slightly sour sauce is perfect for serving with rich meat such as duck, goose and pork.

750 g (1 lb 10 oz) redcurrants, stalks removed
500 g (1 lb 2 oz) granulated sugar
1 strip orange zest
3 cloves
3 allspice berries or large pinch ground
   allspice
150 ml (¼ pint) white balsamic vinegar

1 Put the redcurrants into a large pan or preserving pan along with all the remaining ingredients. Bring slowly to the boil, stirring often until all the sugar has dissolved.

2 Boil for 20–25 minutes. After the shortest cooking time, start checking if the sauce is ready by dragging a channel through the mixture so that the bottom of the pan is visible. If the channel fills immediately with liquid, the sauce is not yet ready. Cook for a further 5 minutes and check again. The sauce is ready when the channel does not fill and the mixture is very thick.

3 Remove from the heat and leave to stand briefly. Carefully pour into hot sterilised jars (page 9). Seal the jars and allow the sauce to cool completely. Label the jars and store the sauce in a cool, dark cupboard for about 1 month before eating.

Passata

Makes: *1 x 500 ml (18 fl oz) jar*
Preparation & cooking time: *2½ hours*

Bottling tomatoes takes some care because they don't contain sufficient acid to prevent the growth of harmful bacteria. There is a very simple solution, however, and that is to add lemon juice to each jar.

2 kg (4 lb 8 oz) ripe plum tomatoes
juice of 1–2 lemons

1 Wash the tomatoes well in cold water. Cut them in half and remove the core and tough white piece in the centre. Remove as many seeds as you can and squeeze out any excess moisture.

2 Put the tomatoes into a large saucepan or preserving pan and cook, uncovered, over a medium-low heat for about 1½–2 hours or until very soft, stirring often and keeping an eye on them to make sure they don't catch.

3 Allow to cool briefly before pressing the mixture through a sieve or food mill (mouli) to remove the skins and any stray seeds. Meanwhile, sterilise the jars and lids (page 9). Put about 1 tablespoon of lemon juice into the bottom of each jar.

4 Using a jam funnel, pour the passata into the prepared jars leaving a gap of about 2 cm (¾ inch) at the top.

5 Replace the lids and place the filled jars into a large deep pan, ensuring that the jars don't touch each other (thread a tea towel between them to keep them apart). Completely cover the jars with water by at least 2.5 cm (1 inch). Bring to the boil and simmer for about 20 minutes. You will see the lids become slightly indented at the tops. This is because a vacuum has now formed between the sauce and the lid.

6 Turn off the heat and leave to cool completely before removing the jars from the water. Dry well then label and store. Keep sealed for up to a year.

Bottled Tomato and Coriander Sauce

Makes: *1 x 500 ml (18 fl oz) jar*
Preparation & cooking time: *2½ hours*

This is a fantastic sauce in the middle of winter – reheat a jar and serve it over pasta for the quickest supper ever.

2 kg (4 lb 8 oz) ripe, preferably plum, tomatoes
1 tablespoon olive oil
2.5 cm (1 inch) piece fresh ginger, grated
1 clove garlic, crushed
3 tablespoons chopped fresh coriander
salt
freshly ground black pepper
juice of 1 lemon

1 Wash the tomatoes well in cold water. Cut them in half and remove the core and tough white piece in the centre. Remove as many seeds as you can and squeeze out any excess moisture.

2 Heat the oil in a large pan. Add the ginger and garlic and cook briefly before adding the tomatoes. Reduce the heat and cook for about 1–1½ hours, stirring often, until the tomatoes are thickened and reduced.

3 Stir in the chopped coriander and season to taste. Meanwhile, sterilise the jars and lids (page 9). Put about 1 tablespoon of lemon juice into the bottom of each jar.

4 Using a jam funnel, pour the sauce into the prepared jars, leaving a gap of about 2.5 cm (1 inch) at the top.

5 Replace the lids and place the filled jars in a large, deep pan, ensuring that the jars don't touch each other (thread a tea towel between them to keep them apart if necessary). Completely cover the jars with water by at least 2.5 cm (1 inch). Bring to the boil and simmer for about 20 minutes. You will see the lids become slightly indented at the tops. This is because a vacuum has now formed between the sauce and the lid.

6 Turn off the heat and leave to cool completely before removing the jars from the water. Dry well then label and store. Keep the sauce sealed for up to 1 year.

Bottled Tomatoes with Basil and Garlic

Makes: *1 x 500 ml (18 fl oz) jar*
Preparation & cooking time: *2½ hours*

Tomatoes and basil were made for each other. Add this sauce to some browned onions and mince then simmer for an hour or so and serve over pasta or as a sauce for lasagne.

2 kg (4 lb 8 oz) ripe tomatoes, preferably plum
3 tablespoons good quality extra virgin olive
    oil
1 clove garlic, crushed
2 tablespoons chopped fresh basil, plus 1 leaf
    for each jar
salt
freshly ground black pepper
juice of 1 lemon

1 Wash the tomatoes well in cold water. Cut them in half and remove the core and tough white piece in the centre. Remove as many seeds as you can and squeeze out any excess moisture.

2 Heat 1 tablespoon of the olive oil in a large pan and add the garlic. Cook briefly, not allowing it to brown, before adding the tomatoes. Bring to the boil and reduce the heat. Cook, uncovered, for about 1–1½ hours, stirring often, until the tomatoes are thickened and reduced.

3 Add the remaining oil and chopped basil and season to taste. Meanwhile, sterilise the jars (page 9). Put about 1 tablespoon of lemon juice into the bottom of each jar.

4 Using a jam funnel, pour the sauce into the prepared jars, leaving a gap of about 2.5 cm (1 inch) at the top. Add one fresh basil leaf to the top of each jar.

5 Replace the lids and place the filled jars into a large, deep pan, ensuring that the jars don't touch each other (thread a tea towel between them to keep them apart if necessary). Completely cover the jars with water by at least 2.5 cm (1 inch). Bring to the boil and simmer for about 20 minutes. You will see the lids become slightly indented at the tops. This is because a vacuum has now formed between the sauce and the lid.

6 Remove the jars from the heat and the water and allow the tomato mixture to cool completely before labelling and storing. Keep the jars sealed for up to 1 year.

Plum Ketchup

Makes: *5 x 500 ml (18 fl oz) jars*
Preparation & cooking time: *3½ hours*

Try this spicy sauce, instead of hoisin, with crispy duck.

2 teaspoons black peppercorns
2 teaspoons mustard seeds
1 cinnamon stick
1 star anise
2.5 cm (1 inch) piece fresh ginger, peeled and
    grated
4 allspice berries
1 clove garlic peeled
1.8 kg (4 lb) plums or damsons, halved and
    stoned
115 g (4 oz) currants
225 g (8 oz) onions, peeled and finely chopped
600 ml (1 pint) distilled white vinegar
1 tablespoon sea salt
1 pinch chilli flakes
350 g (12 oz) demerara sugar

1 Tie the peppercorns, mustard seeds,
cinnamon stick, star anise, ginger, allspice and
garlic in a small muslin bag and set aside.

2 Put the plums, currants, onions, half the
vinegar, salt, chilli flakes and spice bag into a
large pan or preserving pan.

3 Bring to the boil and cook for about 30
minutes, until the plums are very soft. Remove
the bag of spices and set aside. Transfer the
plums to a food processor or blender, or use
a stick blender, and process until very smooth
– if necessary, use a sieve.

4 Return the resulting purée to the pan along
with the bag of spices, remaining vinegar
and sugar. Return to a simmer and cook for
a further 1½–2 hours until very thick, stirring
often to prevent it catching.

5 Using a jam funnel, pour the sauce into
sterilised jars, leaving a gap of about 2 cm
(1 inch) at the top. Replace the lids and place
the filled jars in a large, deep pan, ensuring
that the jars don't touch each other (thread a
tea towel between them to keep them apart
if necessary). Completely cover the jars with
water by at least 2.5 cm (1 inch). Bring to the
boil and simmer for about 20 minutes. You
will see the lids become slightly indented at
the tops. This is because a vacuum has now
formed between the sauce and the lid.

6 Allow to cool completely. Remove the jars
and dry well before labelling and storing. The
ketchup will keep for up to 6 months.

Tomato Ketchup

Makes: *4 x 225 ml (8 fl oz) jars*
Preparation & cooking time: *3 hours*

Less sweet than commercial ketchup, this is a great one for the kids to dip their chips into.

3 kg (6½ lb) ripe tomatoes, roughly chopped
4 medium onions, peeled, halved and sliced
1 large red pepper, de-seeded and white
   filament removed, chopped
75 g (3 oz) soft brown sugar
250 ml (9 fl oz) cider vinegar
½ teaspoon Dijon mustard
1 cinnamon stick
1 teaspoon whole allspice
2 teaspoons whole cloves
2 teaspoons ground mace
2 teaspoons celery seeds
2 teaspoons black peppercorns
1 bay leaf
1 clove garlic, peeled and bruised
salt

1 Combine the tomatoes, onions and pepper in a large, heavy pan over a medium heat and simmer, stirring occasionally, until very soft – about 45 minutes. Transfer to a food processor or blender, or use a stick blender to make a smooth purée. Return the purée to the pan along with the sugar, vinegar and mustard. Tie the spices and garlic in a square of muslin and add it to the pan.

2 Bring the mixture to the boil then reduce to a slow simmer. Continue to cook, allowing it to bubble gently, stirring often and carefully, for about 1–½ hours, until thoroughly blended and quite thick.

3 Press the resulting mixture through a sieve to remove the seeds and any bits of skin. Return to the pan, season to taste and reheat until simmering.

4 Using a jam funnel, pour the sauce into sterilized jars, leaving a gap of about 2.5 cm (1 inch) at the top. Replace the lids and place the filled jars into a large, deep pan, ensuring that the jars don't touch each other (thread a tea towel between them to keep them apart if necessary). Completely cover the jars with water by at least 2.5 cm (1 inch).

5 Bring to the boil and simmer for about 20 minutes. You will see the lids become slightly indented at the tops. This is because a vacuum has now formed between the sauce and the lid.

6 Allow to cool completely. Remove the jars from the water and dry thoroughly before labelling and storing. The ketchup will keep for up to 6 months.

Basil Pesto

Makes: *1 x 225 ml (8 fl oz) jars*
Preparation & cooking time: *10 minutes*

This is not a preserve in the classic sense because it isn't cooked and bottled. The best way to keep pesto for a long time is to freeze it. I transfer the mixture to ice cube trays, open freeze them, then put the cubes into a zip-top bag. I just add cubes straight from the freezer to sauces, or defrost and stir into pasta in the classic way.

2 good handfuls of fresh basil leaves, about
    50 g (2 oz)
2 cloves garlic, crushed
2 tablespoons toasted pine nuts
50 g (2 oz) piece Parmesan cheese, roughly
    chopped or broken
150 ml (¼ pint) good quality extra virgin
    olive oil (plus a little extra for covering
    if necessary)
salt and freshly ground black pepper

1 Put the basil, garlic and pine nuts into the bowl of a food processor and blitz briefly to chop the basil and pine nuts coarsely. Now add the Parmesan pieces and blitz again until the cheese is finely chopped.

2 With the motor running, drizzle in all but a couple of tablespoons of the olive oil. Season to taste. Transfer to an airtight container, add the remaining olive oil to cover (this will help preserve the colour) and refrigerate for up to 2 weeks, or freeze as above.

Tapenade

Makes: *1 x 225 ml (8 fl oz) jar*
Preparation & cooking time: *15 minutes*

Use this spread on crisp, toasted French bread slices and serve with dry sherry as an hors d'oeuvre.

1 clove garlic, crushed
juice of 1 lemon
3 tablespoons capers, chopped
6 anchovy fillets, chopped
250 g (9 oz) pitted black olives, chopped
small bunch fresh parsley, chopped
salt
freshly ground black pepper
4 tablespoons extra virgin olive oil

1 Depending on whether you prefer a coarse or smooth texture, either mix everything together and transfer to an airtight container or put everything except the oil into a food processor and blend until smooth. Then add enough of the oil to make a paste, blend again briefly to mix and transfer the mixture to an airtight container. Top with any remaining oil. Use within 1 week.

Walnut Pesto

Makes: *1 x 225 ml (8 fl oz) jar*
Preparation & cooking time: *10 minutes*

Try adding a little cream to your pasta along with a good scoop of this unusual pesto.

3 tablespoons chopped fresh basil
3 tablespoons chopped fresh parsley
25 g (1 oz) wild rocket leaves
2 cloves garlic, crushed
75 g (3 oz) toasted walnuts
50 g (2 oz) piece Pecorino Romano
  cheese, grated
150 ml (¼ pint) good quality extra virgin olive oil
salt
freshly ground black pepper

1 Put the basil, parsley, rocket, garlic and walnuts into the bowl of a food processor and blitz briefly to chop everything coarsely. Now add the cheese and blitz again until everything is finely chopped.

2 Scrape the sauce into a clean bowl, stir in all but 2 tablespoons of the olive oil and season to taste. Transfer to an airtight container, add the remaining olive oil to cover (this will help preserve the colour) and refrigerate for up to 2 weeks or freeze as for the Basil Pesto (page 127).

Cranberry Sauce

Makes: *1 x 225 ml (8 fl oz) jar*
Preparation & cooking time: *20 minutes*

The classic Christmas turkey accompaniment – ready in only 20 minutes!

175 g (6 oz) caster sugar
5 tablespoons port
zest and juice of 1 orange
375 g (12 oz) cranberries, fresh or frozen
1 eating apple, finely chopped

1 Dissolve the sugar in a medium pan with 4 tablespoons of the port and the orange juice.

2 Stir in the cranberries, apple and orange zest. Cook uncovered for 8–10 minutes (slightly longer if the cranberries are frozen) until the fruit is soft and the juices are thick. Test for a set (page 12) and, if necessary, boil for a further minute then test again. Continue testing at 1-minute intervals, as necessary, until the sauce has reached setting point.

3 Remove from the heat, skim off any scum, and stir in the remaining tablespoon of port. Allow the mixture to cool slightly before carefully pouring into sterilised jars (page 9). Seal the jars and allow the sauce to cool completely before labelling and storing.

Anchoïade

Makes: *1 x 225 ml (8 fl oz) jar*
Preparation & cooking time: *10 minutes*

Anchoïade is a classic anchovy dip, usually made with olives and lots of garlic, but the addition of toasted almonds in this recipe makes it very special. As with a couple of the other sauces in this chapter, it has a short shelf life but can be frozen in ice cube trays (see Basil Pesto, page 127).

2 x 50 g tins anchovy fillets in olive oil,
    drained, oil reserved
4 cloves garlic, crushed
50 g (2 oz) blanched almonds, toasted
50 g (2 oz) pitted green olives
2 tablespoons chopped fresh parsley
2 tablespoons chopped fresh basil
1 teaspoon finely grated lemon zest
2 tablespoons sherry vinegar
150–175 ml (5–6 fl oz) extra virgin olive oil
salt
freshly ground black pepper

1 Put all the ingredients, except the olive oil, salt and freshly ground black pepper, into the bowl of a food processor. Process until everything is finely chopped.

2 Put the olive oil from the anchovies into a measuring jug. Add enough extra virgin olive oil to make 175 ml (6 fl oz).

3 Transfer the mixture from the food processor to a bowl and stir in 150 ml (¼ pint) of the oil, adding more if the mixture seems dry and reserving 2 tablespoons. Season to taste, being careful not to over-salt, as the anchovies and olives will add a fair amount of salt already.

4 Transfer to an airtight container, add the remaining olive oil to cover (this will help preserve the colour) and refrigerate for up to 2 weeks or freeze as for the Basil Pesto (page 127).

Oils, Vinegars and Alcohol

Flavoured oils and vinegars are so easy to make and have their uses – you'll want to have some always to hand for dressing salads. The fruit vinegars, made as they are with fruit purées, are great in their own right as quick sauces for rich and oily meats such as duck and goose. Fruit and alcohol make terrific bedfellows – the traditional Rumtopf recipe here, which takes many months to put together, is well worth the wait to pour over ice cream around Christmastime.

Home-dried Cherry Tomatoes

Makes: *1 x 500 ml (18 fl oz) jar*
Preparation & cooking time: *45 minutes*

These sweet little nuggets are fantastic strewn over a home-made pizza.

1 kg (2 lb 4 oz) ripe cherry tomatoes,
preferably on the vine
fresh thyme
3–4 tablespoons olive oil
salt
freshly ground black pepper
good quality extra virgin olive oil, to pack

1 Preheat the oven to Gas Mark 1/140°C/275°F. Remove the tomatoes from the vine and cut each in half. Lay cut-side up in a single layer on a non-stick baking sheet. Strip the thyme leaves from the stalks and sprinkle over the tomatoes. Drizzle with the olive oil and season with salt and freshly ground black pepper.

2 Transfer to the middle shelf of the oven and cook for about 30 minutes, until well shrivelled but not browned. Remove from the oven and allow the tomatoes to cool completely.

3 Transfer the cooled tomatoes to cold sterilised jars (page 9). Cover completely with olive oil and seal. The tomatoes should keep, unopened and not refrigerated, for several months. Once opened, keep in the fridge and use within 2 weeks.

Semi-dried Plum Tomatoes

Makes: *2 x 500 ml (18 fl oz) jars*
Preparation and cooking time: *1½ hours*

These are delicious chopped in a crisp winter salad. Use a little of the oil in your vinaigrette too.

1 kg (2 lb 4 oz) ripe plum or vine tomatoes
**fresh basil, finely sliced, plus a few whole
   leaves for bottling**
3–4 tablespoons olive oil
salt
freshly ground black pepper
good quality extra virgin olive oil, to pack

1 Preheat the oven to Gas Mark 1/140°C/275°F. Cut the tomatoes in half lengthwise. Lay the tomatoes, cut-side up, in a single layer on a non-stick baking sheet. Sprinkle the sliced basil over the tomatoes. Drizzle with the olive oil and season with salt and freshly ground black pepper.

2 Transfer to the middle shelf of the oven and cook for about 45–55 minutes, until well shrivelled but not browned. Remove from the oven and allow the tomatoes to cool completely.

3 Transfer the cooled tomatoes to cold sterilised jars (page 9), adding a few extra whole basil leaves. Cover completely with olive oil and seal. The tomatoes should keep, unopened and not in the fridge, for several months. Once opened, keep refrigerated and use within 2 weeks.

Marinated Black Olives

Makes: *1 x 500 ml (18 fl oz) jar*
Preparation and cooking time: *10 minutes*

Make all three varieties and serve with Spanish cured ham and bread as part of a tapas platter. Ice-cold fino sherry completes the picture.

200 g (7 oz) black olives
½ preserved lemon (page 107), finely chopped
1 tablespoon finely chopped fresh rosemary
olive oil, to cover

1 Mix together the olives, preserved lemon and rosemary. Add about 3 tablespoons olive oil and mix together well.

2 Transfer the mixture to a 500 ml (18 fl oz) sterilised jar (page 9). Add enough oil to completely cover the olives. Seal, label and set aside to marinate for at least 1 week. Consume within 3 weeks. Refrigerate once opened.

Marinated Green Olives

Follow the recipe above using the following ingredients: 200 g (7 oz) green olives, the juice and finely grated zest of 1 orange, 2 tablespoons of finely chopped mint, 1 teaspoon of toasted cumin seeds, 2 crushed cloves of garlic, 3 tablespoons of olive oil. Pot and cover with olive oil as for black olives.

Marinated Goat's Cheese

Take 1 x 350 g (12 oz) goat's cheese log and cut into four or five pieces to fit a clean 225 ml (8 fl oz) jar. Alternatively, use smaller whole cheeses. Put the cheese pieces into the jar along with 1 tablespoon of lightly crushed mixed peppercorns, 2 crushed cloves of garlic, 2 or 3 bushy sprigs of fresh thyme, a couple of strips of orange zest and 1 whole dried Kashmiri chilli. Cover everything with good quality olive oil, seal and leave to marinate in the refrigerator for at least two days and up to 1 week before using. Keep for up to 2 weeks.

Herb Oil

Makes: *1 x 225 ml (8 fl oz) jar*
Preparation & cooking time: *10 minutes + straining*

Use this recipe for any soft herb, including chives, tarragon, mint and parsley or any combination you prefer. There are many methods for making herb-infused oils but this cold infusion method gives a good, vibrant flavour and colour to the oil.

3 or 4 good handfuls of fresh herbs (as a measure, pack into a measuring jug up to the 600 ml/1 pint mark)
300 ml (½ pint) good quality extra virgin olive oil

1 Bring a large pan of water to the boil. Add the herbs and make sure you submerge them well. Blanch for 5 seconds only. Immediately drain in a colander under cold running water. Drain well and squeeze to remove as much water as possible.

2 Put the herbs and olive oil into a blender or food processor and blend until quite smooth. Strain the mixture through a fine-meshed sieve to remove as many large pieces of herb as possible.

3 Now, either line a fine-meshed sieve with three or four layers of muslin or use a coffee filter paper and coffee filter cone set over a bowl or cup. Pour the oil through the muslin or coffee filter and allow the liquid to drip through at its own pace. Transfer to a sterilised bottle. Cover tightly and keep for 2 weeks in the refrigerator.

Warm Infused Oils

For tough-leaved herbs such as rosemary, thyme, sage and lavender, or for spices like cumin, cinnamon, nutmeg, ginger, star anise or black pepper, measure about 150 ml (¼ pint) volume of finely chopped herbs or about 50 g (2 oz) spices. Put the herbs or spices along with 300 ml (½ pint) good quality extra virgin olive oil into a heavy saucepan. Heat over a high heat until the mixture begins sizzling gently. Strain as step 3 (left) into a clean sterilised bottle or jar, pressing down on the herbs or spices to extract all the oil. Seal tightly and keep for up to 2 weeks in the refrigerator. Makes about 250 ml (9 fl oz).

Fruit Vinegars

Makes: *about 500 ml (18 fl oz)*
Preparation & cooking time: *15 minutes*

I have always found commercial fruit vinegars too harsh. This method of making your own, by blending the fruit with vanilla syrup, produces a sweeter finish with stronger fruity flavours – and it is easier to use in both savoury and sweet recipes. The colour is beautiful, and the vinegars make excellent gifts if decanted to pretty bottles.

200 g (7 oz) granulated sugar
75 ml (3 fl oz) water
1 vanilla pod
400 g (14 oz) ripe raspberries, or 2 large ripe
   mangoes, peeled and diced, or 350 g
   (12 oz) fresh or thawed frozen cranberries
125 ml (4 fl oz) champagne vinegar or white
   wine vinegar

1 First, make the vanilla syrup by putting the sugar, water and vanilla pod into a medium saucepan over a gentle heat. Stir often until the sugar has dissolved, then increase the heat and bring it to the boil. Simmer for 4 minutes, until thick and syrupy.

2 Transfer the syrup to a blender, or use a stick blender, and process the syrup until the vanilla pod is finely chopped. Strain the mixture through a fine sieve then set aside until cold.

3 Put the fruit of your choice into the blender with 125 ml (4 fl oz) of the vanilla syrup and the vinegar. Use any leftover syrup to make another flavour or to poach peaches or pears.

Blend until smooth. Add a little more vinegar if it is too thick (it should pour easily but have some texture).

4 Strain through a fine sieve into a sterilised jar or bottle and seal with a non-metallic lid. Refrigerate for up to 1 month.

Herb Vinegar

Pack fresh green herbs of your choice (e.g. basil, tarragon, lavender flowers and leaves, oregano, mint, sage, chives) up to the 300 ml (10 fl oz) mark in a measuring jug. Transfer to a blender along with 300 ml (10 fl oz) champagne vinegar or white wine vinegar. Blend for about 30 seconds until very finely chopped. Strain the liquid into a sterilised jar or bottle and seal with a non-metallic lid. The colour will change from a vibrant green to a dull brown almost immediately, but this doesn't impair the flavour. Keep in the refrigerator for up to 3 weeks. Makes about 250 ml (9 fl oz).

Rumtopf

Makes: *1 Rumtopf jar*
Preparation & cooking time: *10 minutes (per addition of fruit) + months of macerating*

This is a delicious traditional German recipe for preserving fruits in alcohol and sugar as they come into season. Usually made in a ceramic container made for the purpose (easily found online), you add each fruit in layers then top up with sugar and rum until the last fruit – usually pineapple – is added, around October. The fruits soften and create a thick, syrupy liqueur, which is delicious over ice cream or Greek yoghurt and is ready in time for Christmas. Read the recipe carefully before beginning – making a Rumtopf is not a quick process. You don't need a traditional Rumtopf jar – any large ceramic jar, or even a plastic container with a lid, will do.

To start:
500 g (1 lb 2 oz) strawberries, washed and hulled
500 g (1 lb 2 oz) sugar
dark rum

1 Put the strawberries in the bottom of your Rumtopf and sprinkle over the sugar. Leave overnight until the sugar has dissolved, then add just enough dark rum to cover. If necessary, put a small saucer on top to make sure the fruit stays submerged.

2 Continue to add 500 g (1lb 2 oz) of each summer fruit as they come into season, but add only an additional 250 g (9 oz) sugar per fruit, and always top up with dark rum. Make sure the fruit is always submerged. Keep the pot covered at all times with a layer of cling film as well as the lid to avoid evaporation and flying insects. Do not stir.

Suitable additional fruits include apricots, cherries, grapes, peaches, plums, raspberries, redcurrants, loganberries and pineapple. Fruits should be prepared as they would be for canning – stone fruits should be stoned, but most others can be left whole. Pineapple should be peeled, cored and cubed and usually goes in last.

3 Once the last fruit has been added, leave the pot well covered for at least 6 weeks, preferably for 2–3 months – it is usually ready in time for Christmas. Treat the liquid from the Rumtopf as a liqueur and eat the fruit spooned over ice cream, yoghurt or plain sponge cake.

Note: If the liquid tastes too strongly of rum, give the Rumtopf a stir as the sugar may have settled at the bottom.

Peaches in Brandy

Makes: *1 x 1 litre (1¾ pints) jar*
Preparation & cooking time: *20 minutes*

Serve these warm over ice cream around Christmas-time.

1 kg (2 lb 4 oz) peaches, halved and stoned
500 g (1 lb 2 oz) sugar
1 cinnamon stick
3 cloves
600 ml (1 pint) brandy

1 Put the peaches into a pan with the sugar, cinnamon, cloves and brandy. Place over a low heat until the sugar has melted and the brandy is on the verge of boiling – do not allow the brandy to boil.

2 Remove the pan from the heat. Transfer the fruit to a hot sterilised jar (page 9) and pour over the brandy and spices. Seal, label when cold and set aside for about 1 month before eating.

Cherries in Kirsch

Put 1.5 kg (3 lb 5 oz) sweet cherries into a large bowl and sprinkle with 100 g (3½ oz) sugar. Halve the cherries and pit them if you prefer, although traditionally the pits stay in as they add flavour. Cover and leave overnight. Next day, strain the juices into a bowl and set aside the cherries. Put the juice into a saucepan with ½ cinnamon stick, a vanilla pod and 4 whole cloves. Bring to the boil then remove the pan from the heat. Put the cherries into a warm sterilised jar. Strain the juices and discard the whole spices. Add about 225 ml (8 fl oz) water to the strained juices along with 125 ml (4 fl oz) kirsch and pour this over the cherries to cover – add a little more water if necessary. Seal the jar and store in a cool dark place for about 1 month before using.

Index